Three Mystics Walk into a Tavern

A Once and Future Meeting of Rumi, Meister Eckhart, and Moses de León in Medieval Venice

James C. Harrington and Sidney G. Hall III

Hamilton Books

An Imprint of
Rowman & Littlefield
Lanham • Boulder • New York • Toronto • Plymouth, UK

Copyright © 2015 by Hamilton Books
4501 Forbes Boulevard, Suite 200, Lanham, Maryland 20706
Hamilton Books Aquisitions Department (301) 459-3366

Unit A, Whitacre Mews, 26-34 Stannary Street,
London SE11 4AB, United Kingdom

Library of Congress Control Number: 2014959059
ISBN: 978-0-7618-6542-1 (pbk : alk. paper)—ISBN: 978-0-7618-6543-8 (electronic)

∞™ The paper used in this publication meets the minimum requirements of American
National Standard for Information Sciences Permanence of Paper for Printed Library
Materials, ANSI/NISO Z39.48-1992.

We respectfully thank all those people in our lives, family and friends, and those who went before us, some of whom appear in this book, for their efforts and commitment to lighting the "Divine Spark" within us, and generations to come, so that it manifest itself in us as life, justice, and equality. To them, we dedicate this book.

We also express our thanks to Rolando Pérez for his superb editing assistance and helpful insights, which we incorporated into this book.

Contents

Foreword

Ori Z. Soltes

In the very beginning of the 12th century, the renowned Muslim jurist al-Ghazali (1058–1111) found himself frustrated. As a professor of jurisprudence at the University of Baghdad since the age of 35, he was at somewhat of a spiritual and intellectual dead-end. He had come to realize that he could never prove the validity of the Qur'an's verses to the satisfaction of a sceptic—to say nothing of a non-believer—by means of the detailed rational arguments that he had been devising over the years. For he came to understand that, while the precepts of faith may be bolstered for the believer in reasonable arguments that are *formally* rational, such arguments ultimately all circle back to their own beginnings in the faith without which they fall apart.

Al-Ghazali thought, however, that there must be—and soon came to realize that there was—another path to spiritual satisfaction besides the path of *shari'a* and its emphasis on logical, very intellectual argumentation. That path was (and is) the Muslim mystical path known as Sufism. Al-Ghazali the legal scholar left his university position and his friends and family and went off to join a group of Syrian Sufis. He devoted the last ten years of his life to exploring and explaining the precepts of a form of Islam that was *experiential* in its shape, in which anyone and everyone who genuinely desired to do so—whether of lower or upper socio-economic condition, whether schooled or unschooled in the exegetical ideas that flourished in the mosques and madrasas—could *find* God, *feel* God: become, if even for only a moment, *one with the One*.

The mystical idea—of a deeper, more hidden depth to Divinity, which, by pure paradox, can and yet cannot (cannot and yet can) be accessed—can draw and has drawn any number of individuals along its path. No religious tradition is without its mystical side, for ultimately religion addresses a realm beyond our own; and all human groups express an interest in that realm. Within every tradition, the mystics seek more emphatically, more intensely for still greater depths within that Other than everyday religion seems to seek. This is the path that Al-Ghazali and many others have ultimately sought along to find—possibly, hopefully—the divine hiddenness that they know is there, even as one can never *know* in the conventional sense anything about divinity, much less about that hiddenness.

Al-Ghazali and the Sufis, who tutored his thinking in new, unshackled directions would have reveled in the intriguing text that follows this foreword. He would surely suggest that it will be of interest and of use to four kinds of people. Those who want a clear and concise yet sufficiently detailed introduction to the world of the 11th through 14th centuries in Europe and Asia—a sweeping sense of what was happening spiritually and culturally across those many miles and decades—will find parts of this volume revelationary. Those who want a concise, clear and sufficiently detailed introduction to the lives and thought of three extraordinary mystics, one from each of the Abrahamic traditions, will find in parts of this volume essential starting points toward an ongoing dialogue with any or all of them. Their revolutionary contributions to the history of thought, and not only to the history of mystical aspiration, are stunning, and carefully discussed in this volume.

Those who appreciate the fantasy of three important historical figures who never met and may well never even have heard about each other—it is we who, from the lens of many centuries of distance are able to focus on their points of overlap and divergence—but who, had they met, might well have enjoyed an extraordinary conversation, will find the heart of this volume immensely pleasurable. That heart transforms intellectual discussions into intuitive, imagination-lush experiences of the minds of these figures. One might say that the first aspect of the volume is like *Pshat*, the second like *Remez* and the third like *Drash*, in the standard rabbinic approach to the exegesis of God's word.

The fourth—ideal—reader is like the fourth approach to God's word: *Sod*. Such a reader, indeed, is like Rabbi Akiva entering the *PaRDeS*, in comparison with the three other rabbis who enter with him but don't "go in peace and return in peace," as he does. That reader is the one who wants and appreciates all three of these elements and how they offer three different modes of exegesis of the human yearning for and striving toward God through God's words and the ever-complicating reality of human words.

For this volume interweaves, in a fascinating and magisterial manner, the straightforward double intellectual thread of general history and culture with biographical information and an account of the spiritual contributions and legacies of Jalal ad-Din Rumi, Meister Eckhart and Moses de León. As if that richness of presentation were not sufficient, the authors have engaged these three characters in a casual imagined conversation about not so casual subjects—beginning, no less, with God. The authors tease out perspectives from their heroes in conversation that do two important things. They reveal in a more intimate, experiential way the kinds of thoughts that these three mystics either expressed in what they wrote or *might* have thought but never wrote—perhaps never spoke—at least in what has survived to our own time from their own writings and writings about them. We are thus confronted with a perfect paradox: the authors have given *voice* to the apophatic side of these three mystics who spent their adult lives wrestling with the Ineffable One.

So the conversation offers a perfectly logical shape that defies everyday logic (as mysticism itself must do and does): a shape that encompasses thinkers not only before the time of this trio but those who have come after. All three move thinkers comfortably from the Apostle Paul and Ibn al-Arabi to Dostoevsky and Jackson Browne. Those who come after include figures from *our own time*, the 21st century.

And so, two things happen. The first is that the conversation inherently and naturally transcends ordinary time and space. A world of ideas emanates from the singular time and place of their meeting in the fictional Alighieri Tavern in Venice—*out* to other times and places about which these mystics somehow *know*. As such, they exemplify the timeless and spaceless form of the Source of all Being that expands at the beginning of time and space (as we limited humans understand these properties) to reify the universe—and the mystical experience itself of seeking oneness with that Source, in the form, and not only the content, of their conversation.

The second is that the reader cannot help but join in the conversation, and not only because it *is* a conversation and not a treatise, a dialogue and not a lecture. We join in because the conversation talks to the conditions and issues of today, in part through voices that speak today, in the present tense, and not only those that speak out of some misty distant past.

The threads of this volume are woven together in a richly hued, tight and very readable tapestry. The tapestry is also a doorway—into the warmest of intellectual and spiritual taverns, into which all of us are invited, out of the dark, windy night of the everyday world and its complications. The wise reader will enter the doorway, responding to the universalist words, such as Rumi offered, that blossom throughout the narrative—that are carved over the doorway and woven into the tapestry. The wise reader will read, beginning to end, hardly stopping for breath, inspired to

> Come…,
> Whoever you are.
> Religious, infidel, heretic, or pagan.
> Even if you promised a hundred times,
> And a hundred times you broke your promise,
> This door is not the door
> Of hopelessness and frustration.
> This door is open for everybody.
> Come, come as you are.

Introductory Comments — A Tavern?

Come, let us pass this pathway over
that which to the tavern leads;
there waits the wine, and there the door,
which every traveler needs.

—Hafez, Ghazal 34

This book had its genesis on the patio of the Nomad neighborhood bar in Austin, Texas, during a discussion over a few beers about mystics: how was it that Jalal ad-Din Rumi, Meister Eckhart, and Moses de León, three great mystics with enormous impact in their respective religious traditions, emerged about the same time in history, with similar mystical impulses, but without knowing of each other?

Was this a fluke or a product of history? Did they just happen by chance to point those around them (and us, more broadly) in a similar spiritual direction? Did they represent a certain stage in human progression or manifest a common current that ran deep within humankind at the time, but below surface—separate wells of the same mighty Underground River, as Eckhart would have it?

We began to tinker with the idea of writing about this, mostly out of intellectual curiosity, and how a fantasy dialog among the three mystics might go. The more we talked, however, the more we focused on the thought that such a dialog might be helpful to individuals in search of a deeper spiritual life, especially in light of the sharp decline in people's religious affiliation and the rising number of persons exploring alternative spiritual paths. Thus, this book has come to see the light of day.

This is not a call to "return" to church, synagogue, or mosque, but a suggestion that there are many wells from which to draw on one's spiritual journey. We also hope to speak to the spiritually curious with no religious affiliation. For those of a religious tradition or estranged from one, we might gently suggest there might be useful tools deep in that tradition that could be used for discovering the mystery that may lie deep within.

Should some find the book title somewhat odd, we only note that taverns were common meeting places of medieval travelers for food, drink, conversation, and lodging. Nor did Eckhart or de León live in abstemious cultures. And many of Rumi's poems speak of wine and even of a tavern, but in transcendent terms, often to mean being intoxicated with the Beloved or with "the madness of love" for the Beloved.

> Because of your love.
> I have lost my sobriety.
> I am intoxicated
> by the madness of love.
> . . . .
> In this fog.
> I have become a stranger to myself.
> I am so drunk . . .
> I have lost the way to my house
> . . . .
> In the garden.
> I see only your face.
> From trees and blossoms,
> I inhale only your fragrance.
> . . . .
> Drunk with the ecstasy of love,
> I can no longer tell the difference
> between drunkard and drink,
> between Lover and Beloved. [1]

Exactly to the point, then, the title represents our efforts to recognize and encourage mysticism as part of one's daily, earthly existence, and not something reserved solely to people living on the other side of cloister walls.

Although we wrote about three men of different Abrahamic religious traditions (Jewish, Muslim, and Christian), males have no unique claim on mysticism. Indeed, we also discuss some well-respected women mystics with enormous influence on their peers and those who followed after them. Rabi'a al-'Adawiya of Basra, Hildegard of Bingen, and Marguerite Porete, for example, are stars in the firmament.

The historical concurrence of de León, Rumi, and Eckhart was of interest because of our own personal backgrounds and studies. The same is true as to our focus on the three Abrahamic traditions. There are mystics of all traditions, and of no tradition. Our focus means nothing more, and nothing less.

We disclaim any original scholarship, though we hope our book does give rise to original insights by the reader. Our effort here is to help make the ideas and thought of mysticism—and mysticism itself, especially of the apophatic kind, more accessible to 21st-century individuals.

For the person seeking more in-depth knowledge of mysticism, especially in a historical context, we suggest two excellent scholarly books, from which we admittedly drew immense insight and sometimes sought to paraphrase in more basic terms: *Mysticism in Judaism, Christianity, and Islam: Searching for Oneness* by Ori Z. Soltes; and *Mystical Languages of Unsaying* by Michael A. Sells. Both books are rich in footnotes and bibliographies, and we highly commend them.[2]

This book provides an ample traditional bibliography, but we would draw attention to chapter endnotes that often point to YouTube presentations and web-accessible information, as well as other books, that supplement the bibliography.

We tried our best to use inclusive language and minimize male pronouns; but the truth of the matter is that so many writings of the era with which we are concerned express themselves in male images and pronouns. This often happens in works by women mystics, also. And the word "mystic" itself, although used freely by the three conversationalists, was not a descriptive word in their era of the kind it is in our times; the term is of relatively modern coinage.

We have tried our utmost for maximum fidelity to the respective mystic's own teaching when presenting that person's conversation. Despite considerable hours devoted to exploring and understanding other faith traditions, your authors admit greater familiarity with their Christian backgrounds.

If at times the weight of perspective might seem to lean toward Christianity, we encourage our readers to bring with them the richness of their experience and understanding in their own tradition to restore balance. We firmly believe that all religious traditions and experiences of mystical union draw upon the same Source. Being in the Mystery includes an openness to dialog with other traditions and with each other.

The authors have set up a website about and for the book. It includes web links to the various YouTube videos and websites referenced in the endnotes: www.threemystics.com. The site will also maintain an ongoing updated select bibliography, for which the authors welcome suggestions from the reader.

One last comment. There is no factual basis for the meeting in the Venice tavern. Although the three mystics lived, taught, and wrote in roughly the same era, they never met. Nor is there any reason to believe they even knew of each other. But whether there is an ultimate reality to the meeting is up to the reader to decide.

Not only is this evening and night-long dialog among the three mystics without historical foundation; but they have a certain clairvoyance to predict what will happen, and has happened, in the future; and they will discuss—

and meet—mystics and writers who came before them and will come after them, even in the 20th and 21st centuries. As such, it is always a challenge to effectively reference past, present, and future events and verb tenses consistently in a dialog of this kind about a subject that transcends time. We ask for the reader's understanding of our effort to summon the timeless essence of mysticism, as well as for our chronological creativity.

While the conversation among the three mystics is what we wish to be the focus of this book, the intervening chapters about each of their lives and general thought should be helpful to better understanding their interactive conversations. And there is a chapter with an overview of the era in which they lived. Those chapters are for background and resource, at whatever juncture the reader may wish to consult them, although one new to the mysticism of Jalal ad-Din Rumi, Moses de León, and Meister Eckhart might find them helpful to read before the dialogs.

We hope this book will present an introduction to mysticism, such that it might inspire others to want to move deeper into this Mystery, a mystery that is as accessible to all of us as the sun that brings light to day and the moon upon which we gaze in wonder.[3]

NOTES

1. Rumi, *53 Secrets from the Tavern of Love: Poems from the Rubiayat of Mevlana Rumi*, trans. Amin Banani and Anthony A. Lee (Islamic Encounter Series) (Ashland, OR: White Cloud Press, 2014). Rumi (Robert Filippo, reader), Oct. 23, 2011, "The Drunkards and The Tavern," https://www.youtube.com/watch?v=I8fyCGyrpGk; "The Tavern of the Soul," *Spiritual . . . But Not Religious*, Feb. 28, 2011, http://spiritualnotreligious.blogspot.com/2011/02/tavern-of-soul.html. For another example of Rumi speaking of being "tipsy" and "drunk with love," see *Goodreads*, http://www.goodreads.com/quotes/115470-what-can-i-do-muslims-i-do-not-know-myself.

2. Both books are in the bibliography and are cited throughout.

3. For a beautiful and artistic rendition of Bruce Cockburn's "Mystery," see PainterofPaint, "Bruce Cockburn ~ Mystery," Oct. 29, 2009, https://www.youtube.com/watch?v=4zlZLo3jWZg.

Chapter One

What This Book Is—And Is Not—About

Deep has called unto deep,
and all things have vanished into unity.
The waves and the ocean have become one.
Nothing can come, and nothing can pass away.

—Tukaram

Mysticism is a direct, immediate experience of divinity or of ultimate reality. For many religious seekers, it is the definitive goal of spirituality; but countless people, who are not religious at all, have had mystical experiences.

The term "mysticism" derives from the Greek word "to conceal" in the sense of the hidden. The word, while narrow in definition, has come to apply to a worldwide range of religious traditions and practices. A mystic seeks and finds the Hidden or, as some would state it more aptly, the Hidden finds the mystic, who is in search of the Hidden.

Generally, mysticism rests on the belief that union with, or absorption into, the Deity, the Infinite, God, the Absolute, or the spiritual apprehension of knowledge inaccessible to the intellect, may come to an individual through contemplation and self-surrender.

Whether someone's mystical experience is understood as extra-ordinary or a sense of the sacred within the profane, mystical union is simply "the moment in which the boundaries between divine and human, self and other, melt away."[1] Bede Griffiths, a 20th-century mystic, describes a gloaming moment from his experience:

> Everything then grew still as the sunset faded and the veil of dusk began to cover the earth. I remember now the feeling of awe which came over me. I felt inclined to kneel on the ground, as though I had been standing in the presence

5

of an angel; and I hardly dared to look on the face of the sky, because it seemed to me as though it was but a veil before the face of God . . . . I was suddenly made aware of another world of beauty and mystery such as I had never imagined to exist, except in poetry. It was as though I had begun to see and smell and hear for the first time. The world appeared to me as Wordsworth describes it with "the glory and freshness of a dream."[2]

The three Abrahamic traditions we discuss all share a common sentiment that successful mystics possess a kind of knowledge beyond normative or prescribed knowledge. It is akin to the knowledge possessed by the prophets, which "connects them to the innermost, hidden recess of God."[3] Mystical spiritually for all three traditions "embraces complexity, paradox, and contradiction"[4]; it is poetry, rather than prose.

EVERYONE CAN BE A MYSTIC

Most of us do not think of ourselves as a mystic or a potential mystic. We tend to view mystics as special persons who have had extra-ordinary, out-of-this-world experiences, such as historical figures like the Apostle Paul, Julian of Norwich, or Black Elk.

While a few people experience mysticism in this extra-ordinary way, the majority of us never have such dramatic encounters. Sometimes, it is simply the moment—the beautiful instant when we turn in awe to observe the light of the sunset streaming across water, an uplifting piece of music, a moving YouTube production, a rock concert, attending a masterful theater performance, dancing, or the sense of complete union with a partner in making love.

We believe everybody can become a mystic. Many individuals already are, probably more people than we can imagine. You may not pursue it or even realize it; but mystical experience is not reserved for the pious or the super-religious. As Andrew Harvey, scholar and teacher of mystic traditions, explains it:

> . . . the word *mystic* may mislead or intimidate some people—the prestige accorded to it has traditionally been so exalted that they feel such heightened perception and joy belong to and are attainable by only a few chosen human beings. This is far from the case. Mystical experience is always available— like the divine grace it is—to any who really want it; and all human beings are given in the course of their lives glimpses into the heart of the real which they are free to pursue or forget.[5]
>
> . . . .
>
> When we are touched by mystic grace and allow ourselves to enter its field without fear, we see that we are all parts of a whole, elements of an universal harmony, unique, essential and sacred notes in a divine music that everyone and everything is playing together with us in God and for God.[6]

Mystical union is for everybody, not just for specialists. Mystical experience is beholding the extra-ordinary within the ordinary, to flow freely between the thin place separating our mundane routines from the experiences of the holy. It is "the presence of an almost unfathomable mystery . . . which seems to be drawing me to itself."[7] It is about the paradox of emptying ourselves and thus realizing fulfillment, or, perhaps better, having fulfillment overtake us, not as something sought, but as something that happens.

RESTLESS HEARTS

Augustine of Hippo's famous saying that "our hearts are restless until they rest in thee" may be as descriptive of many people's spiritual journeys in today's world as it was of his in the 4th century. Certainly, many contemporary folks experience a deep spiritual yearning, which they do not feel fulfilled by organized religion or the tradition in which they grew up. There is a sense of estrangement "from the inner ground of meaning and love," as Thomas Merton phrases it, which accompanies this yearning.[8]

To try to deal with their longing and alienation, people may go from one formal religious tradition to another, experimenting, changing congregations, or eventually end up with a newly-formed spiritual community or New Age group. Or they may just search for an individualized spirituality of their own. Searching is always a good sign.

Organized religion has contributed to this gnawing alienation and emptiness with its concentration on dogmatic language, prescribed normative conduct, rote ritual, blind adherence to structures, and so on. These pseudo-priorities have pushed aside what should be the quintessential purpose of religion, to seek and encourage union with "the sacred," however "the sacred" unfolds to us, and union with our human community.

Diana Butler Bass has noted, "American faith has undergone a profound and extensive reorientation away from externalized religion toward internalized spiritual experience." In 1962, she notes, pollsters found that 22 percent of Americans claimed a "mystical experience" of God. By 2009, 48 percent, more than double, confessed a mystical experience with the Divine.[9] During the same period, the number of churchgoers dropped almost as dramatically. People are speaking with their hearts and feet—longing for spirituality, but not finding it in organized religion.[10]

Matthew Fox, a Creation Spirituality theologian, says it this way: "The gap between religion and spirituality is growing ever wider and deeper. Religion appears to have less and less to do with the Spirit, courage, joy, youthfulness, love, or compassion. And more and more people see this and recognize it. Is it at all possible to bridge the chasm and renew religion by renewing worship and offering spiritual praxis?"[11]

We hope this book will be of some help in addressing Fox's quandary and speaking to those whom Bass has identified as mysticism candidates. As scholar, monk, and social activist Wayne Teasdale framed it, "The new spirituality is a spirituality of illuminating our daily lives with what we call the divine and recognizing that in ourselves."[12] It is, as the Little Prince observes, "only with the heart that one can see rightly."[13]

The purpose of this book is not to suggest a new path or conversion or to produce another academic tome. Rather, it is to look deeply at various mystical traditions or impulses from which we can draw to strengthen and perhaps even make deeper use of the religious tradition into which we were born or to which we may have traveled, if any. Or be a book for those who just simply want to embark upon a path to mysticism without religious affiliation. Making the journey is what is important.

We do not desire to homogenize mystical experiences or traditions, or diminish what differentiates them, but to honor and celebrate the differences and find enrichment and guidance in them. There is interconnectedness, to be sure. That, and why we need the interconnectedness, is what this book is about.

Now, it is time to join Jalal ad-Din Rumi, Moses de León, and Meister Eckhart at the tavern in Venice on Sunday, June 13, 1300 (Julian calendar), in late afternoon . . . .

NOTES

1. Michael A. Sells, *Mystical Languages of Unsaying* (Chicago: University of Chicago, 1994), 7.
2. Ibid., ix.
3. Ori Z. Soltes, *Mysticism in Judaism, Christianity, and Islam: Searching for Oneness* (Lanham, MD: Rowman & Littlefield, 2009), 84.
4. Ibid., 88.
5. *The Essential Mystics: The Soul's Journey into Truth*, ed. Andrew Harvey (San Francisco: HarperSanFrancisco, 1996), x.
6. Ibid., xi.
7. Ibid., x.
8. Thomas Merton, *Choosing to Love the World: On Contemplation*, ed. Jonathan Montaldo (Louisville, CO: Sounds True, 2008), 22–23.
9. Diana Butler Bass, *Christianity after Religion: The End of Church and the Birth of a New Spiritual Awakening* (New York: HarperOne, 2013), 3–4.
10. There are four recent books on this topic: Lillian Daniel, *When "Spiritual but Not Religious" Is Not Enough: Seeing God in Surprising Places, Even the Church* (New York: Jericho Books, 2014); Linda A. Mercadante, *Belief without Borders: Inside the Minds of the Spiritual but not Religious*, New York: Oxford University Press, 2014); Thomas Moore, *A Religion of One's Own: A Guide to Creating a Personal Spirituality in a Secular World* (New York: Gotham, 2014); Courtney Bender, *The New Metaphysicals: Spirituality and the American Religious Imagination* (Chicago: University Of Chicago Press, 2010).
11. Matthew Fox, *Confessions: The Making of a Postdenominational Priest* (San Francisco: HarperSanFrancisco, 1991), 244. Fox studied under French theologian Marie-Dominique Chenu, one of the first to "name" a creation-based theology. See John R. Mabry, 1995, "Uncover-

ing the Creation Spirituality Tradition: Chenu and Fox," http://www.apocryphile.org/jrm/articles/cstradition.html.

12. Wayne Teasdale, *The Mystic Hours: A Daybook of Inspirational Wisdom and Devotion* (Novato, CA: New World Library, 2004), 347.

13. Antoine de Saint-Exupery, *The Little Prince* (Waterville, ME; Thorndike Press, 2005), chap. XXI.

Chapter Two

They Meet at
Taverna degli Alighieri in Venice

*A person's true wealth
is the good he or she does in this world.*

—Muhammad

Jalal ad-Din Rumi: Hello, Gentlemen, good evening. You must be Meister Eckhart; and you, Rabbi Moses de León? My apologies for arriving a bit late past our meeting time for dinner. My boat landed just a few hours ago, and I fell asleep in my room upstairs. I had to detour around Greece because of the warfare there. When will we ever learn how fighting interferes with the Lover?

Meister Eckhart: No problem, Mevlana Rumi. I am very pleased to meet you. They told us you had arrived. We are glad you made it. Here, please sit and try some of this *salmo cettii*; it is excellent. This tavern's smoked Mediterranean trout is supposed to be some of Venice's best.

Moses de León: Indeed. I sampled some last night when I arrived. Virtually as good as any I have tasted in my travels around al-Ándalus.

And, thank you, Meister Eckhart, for your kind invitation, bringing us together for this intriguing endeavor with a Christian, Muslim, and me, a Jew, to share our thoughts about mysticism—always a fascinating topic that sometimes has our respective religious authorities breathing down our necks. The words "mystic" and "mysticism" are not familiar terms in our era; they will be of relatively modern vintage. But it is convenient for us to use them, however, to reflect the spiritualities and religious impulses we are discussing.

I regret we could not meet in Jerusalem, as we had hoped. It is a holy city for the three of us; but it is again mired in war and conflict, as it often has been in the past and will be in the future. It is so ironic and sad that people fight over such a sacred city, killing one another and destroying the holy sites in the name of religion. But at least we were able to find a peaceful place in Venice. And picking the Summer Solstice for our rendezvous is a perfect day.

Eckhart: My pleasure. I first heard about you, Rabbi Moses, when I was at the University of Paris and then later from a rabbi or two on a previous visit here in Venice to confer with my Dominican colleagues. And this is also where I learned about you, Mevlana, from some Seljuk merchants, I think from the Sultanate of Rûm. We are delighted you come from the Sufi mysticism tradition of Islam.

Rumi: Ah! Here's the fish, warm bread, and some pasta. A hearty meal would do us good. We have much to discuss. Thanks to Rabbi Moses, we have narrowed the topics down to "God," community, women, religion, and, projecting ahead, why mysticism is important in the 21st century. Not that "narrow" is apropos of any of the themes we have chosen.

Let us pause, ask our landlord to brew up a large pot of the *çay* tea I brought with me, and let our readers review the next few chapters on mysticism generally, the period of history in which we live, and our personal backgrounds—or skip directly to Chapter 8, if they prefer, where our conversation picks up again. They can always visit the intervening chapters later, but looking over them at this juncture might be helpful to a mysticism initiate in following our conversation.

Chapter Three

Mysticism

For Everyone?

And you?
When will you begin that long journey into yourself?

—Rumi

TRYING TO DEFINE THE INDEFINABLE

Mysticism generally, as already noted, is a direct, immediate experience of divinity or ultimate reality. The word *mysticism* derives from the Greek *mystikos*, and, as theologian Matthew Fox notes, has two essential meanings: "to shut one's senses" and "to enter the mysteries."[1] The two are interrelated because only when we shut out the distractions from all the stimuli around us can we be open to mystery.[2]

There are two common kinds of mysticism: kataphatic and apophatic. "Kataphatic" mysticism has content; it uses words, images, symbols, ideas. It expresses God or the Divine through positive terminology. The word "kataphatic" is formed from two Greek words, which roughly translate as bringing God to us in such a way so as to speak of God.

"Apophatic" mysticism, on the other hand, has no content. It means emptying the mind of words and ideas about God and simply resting in God's presence. Centering prayer, for example, which is contemplative prayer or listening prayer, is a type of apophatic mystical practice. "Apophatic" mysticism is sometimes referred to as "negative theology," "unsaying," or "deconstruction" because one of its central tenets is that, by definition, human language limits God, our understanding God, and our ultimate ability to be in mystical union with God. As profound, rich, and imaginative as human speech may be, it is fundamentally limited and limiting.

Apophatic mysticism recognizes it is impossible to name the transcendent or ascribe attributes. To do so is to make the transcendent or divine into a thing, *some-thing*, to anthropomorphize it. But it is *no-thing*; yet, the finite nature of language attempts to say what cannot be said. Even the description of it as an "it" betrays the transcendent nature of beyond thing-ness. Thus, any saying of the Divine must be unsaid. As such, we are in "linguistic regress. Each statement—positive or 'negative'—reveals itself as in need of correction."[3]

Generally, even practitioners of "kataphatic" mysticism have as their quintessential goal a kind of apophatic mystical union with the Divine. Both forms of mysticism involve an idea of self-surrender, although in the apophatic sense it means annihilation of the false ego and letting God unfold and act inside and through the mystic.

This book is about apophatic mysticism. Apophatic mysticism is adoration and a mysticism that also leads to healing and re-building the community.

Celtic spirituality speaks of the apophatic experience as crossing through a veil, a "thin place," between the reality of our everyday lives and the eternal or transcendent. The Celts believed this thin veil separates us from our ancestors and other spirits, who have crossed to the other side. On particular occasions, however, at certain times in the wheel of the year, during meaningful ritual (such as communion, contemplative prayer, music), or in the moment of a sunset, or even in times of sickness and delirium, we cross more easily through the veil.

We observe this same thinking in the renowned medieval Sufi mystic, Ibn al-'Arabi. Commenting on the similarity of al-'Arabi's theology with Jewish mystics of the time, Ori Soltes writes, "As close as the mystic may get to God's innermost core, it remains a *mysterion* because there always remains a veil, however infinitesimally thin, that separates even the most profoundly successful devotee from it."[4]

Marion Zimmer Bradley's classic *The Mists of Avalon* paints a powerful image of mystical union, where one crosses through the veil. Bradley narrates the tale of Arthur of Camelot through the lenses of Morgaine, Arthur's half-sister, and Viviane, who is the Lady of the Lake and High Priestess of Avalon.[5]

As people traverse through the mist, back and forth between the mainland and Avalon, they cross through a veil from one dimension to another. From the mainland to Avalon, they cross into the realm of the sacred; from Avalon to the mainland, they cross back from the holy into the ordinariness of their lives (*profanus*, the profane, the non-sacred).

Certain navigators of rafts are specially equipped, like priests and priestesses, to lead travelers through the veil. Without their assistance, one could become forever lost, stuck and adrift in the mist, never passing through the veil, thus never experiencing the extraordinary in the ordinary, the Divine. Such navigators are often necessary guides or companions.

One could understand crossing through the mist as akin to worship or ritual, but it is also an anthropomorphic way of portraying the pathway toward mystical union. The goal of mystical union is not to remain permanently in a state of bliss, but to take back one's experience of the holy so that it may transform one's life and transform the community.

MYSTICISM BACK ON STAGE

The last twenty-five years have witnessed a resurgent interest in mysticism. When we, the authors, were in seminary (Jim in the 1960s and Sid in the early 1980s), mainstream theological circles viewed mysticism as suspect. While prayer, described as the successive path of meditation, contemplation, and mystical union, was taught, aspiring to the extra-ordinary mysticism of people like the Apostle Paul, Joan of Arc, John of the Cross, or Julian of Norwich, was a dubious venture.

Instead, we learned a systematic theology, rooted in objective principles, methodology, and post-Enlightenment rationalism. Whether one attended a Catholic seminary (like Jim) or a Methodist seminary (like Sid), we studied the theology of giants like Paul Tillich, Rudolf Bultmann, Reinhold Niebuhr, Hans Küng, and Edward Schillebeeckx, but not about the mystery of mysticism.

There is great worth in traditional theological training. Being well-versed in 19th and 20th-century theology is invaluable; but ignoring, or even discounting, mysticism leaves a huge gap in that education.

The closest most of us got to an acceptable mysticism was the psychology of Carl Jung (who spoke of God as the Collective Unconscious) and the ethic of Martin Buber (who saw God in the I-Thou relationship), which were wonderful, but never touched upon the rich experiences of mystical sages across the millennia.

Since mysticism was mostly perceived as a supra-sensual or supernatural experience "beyond" science, there was little room for its exploration in a rationalist theological framework. Part of the reason mysticism was suspect in Western theological education was its popularized association with the performances of mediums, who summoned departed spirits, and the ecstasies of the saints, blissfully portrayed in art and literature as anything but typically human. In addition, many model mystics, especially in church history, performed severe bodily mortification (in Latin, literally, "to put to death") as part of their spiritual practice.

With the advent of the psychology of self-actualization in the 1960s and a different understanding of the mysticism dynamic, mysticism connected to bodily mortification and excessive self-denial was seen as harmful rather than helpful. Not only could it have serious health consequences; but it had the inherent danger of causing ego-building (a potential for ego-centered heroism), instead of being ego-diminishing. Moreover, a theology that did not recognize passion, the body, and sensuality as a part of the divine gift came to be understood as an unacceptable practice of mysticism.

Mystics like Hildegard of Bingen, Meister Eckhart, Moses Maimonides, Ibn al-'Arabi, Moses de León, and Jalal al-Din Rumi, whom contemporary theological schools had studiously ignored, were rediscovered. These mystics, instead of denying their senses, understood mystical union as returning, or backing up, "to the primal sacrament, the primal mystery that is the universe itself . . . call[ing] for a spiritual awakening to the mystery of the universe and our existence in it." For them, "Reentering that mystery [was] a fundamentally holy act, a sacred discipline."[6]

Hence the need for reevaluating mysticism's true meaning and restating that it is about union with the Absolute, and nothing more. The mystic is the person who attains to this union, not the person who only talks about it. To *Be* is the mark of the real initiate.[7]

ONE RIVER, MANY WELLS

Meister Eckhart brilliantly describes God as "a mighty underground river that no one can dam up, and no one can stop." This powerful image depicts the river's flow as independent of humans or even human consciousness. It is also striking that the river is the primary source, the Ultimate Reality, and not the wells from which we may draw.

Mysticism is everywhere. There are many wells among all people and in all religions, even while some of those traditions may cloak the mystical union experience within their own history, ritual, mythology, and even geography. Mystical union is unique and specific to one's own tradition and experience. Yet, while each experience is distinctive, it is also inherently universal.

To offer a personal example of one of the authors, when Sid was a teenager, spending summers in northern Michigan with his grandparents, he witnessed an amazing Aurora Borealis light show. His experience was one of awe and wonder. It was not just seeing the Northern Lights, but also feeling connected to everything in the universe, being linked with God.

The Northern Lights experience is certainly a universal experience, something people from an array of traditions could encounter. However, while the experience was universal, one's specific path, as it relates to the experience, is defined by tradition, history, localized myth, and geography.

Religion, for most of us, depends on our family background, where we were born and grew up. Continuing with the example of Sid's encounter, when he described his sense of the happening to his grandmother the next morning, her response, delivered in her typical Midwestern directness, was, "Aren't the Northern Lights beautiful? Sidney Boy, when you grow up you are going to be a Methodist minister," which is exactly what happened. Had his grandmother been a Pagan, a Native American medicine woman, or Greek Orthodox, her response of which shamanic path Sid should take would have been drawn from a different well, but from the same river.

Religious historian Mircea Eliade observed that all ancient cultures practiced rituals that represented movement from the profane (non-sacred) to the sacred, in which an individual becomes detached "from profane time and magically re-enters the Great Time, the sacred time."[8] These myths and rituals of indigenous communities, which provided the foundational rhythm for modern religion, created the experience of what Eliade called the "eternal return," stepping temporarily out of ordinary time and into "sacred time."

This added meaning to life and a "break" from an otherwise harsh existence. This break could be spontaneous, such as witnessing a brilliant lightning storm or the result of a designed ritual, such as a Native American sweat lodge, Aboriginal walkabout, or Sufi dance. Even though contemporary practitioners of religion sometimes regard themselves as more sophisticated than our ancestors, meaningful myth-making today puts us in touch with these same core rhythms.

Just as a mosque, synagogue, or church, for example, constitutes a break in the profane (non-sacred) space of a current-day city, the service (myth-making) celebrated inside also marks a break in profane temporal duration. "Sacred space" could even be a special location in the woods, on the beach, in the desert for individual contemplation, or where one does yoga or dance.

To enter sacred space in the Christian context, it ". . . is no longer today's historical time that is present—the time experienced, for example, in the adjacent streets—but the time in which the historical existence of Jesus occurred, the time sanctified by his preaching, by his passion, death, and resurrection."[9] The same "sacred" space and time breakaway is true of a place of religious assembly for any tradition and its own rituals.

There always has been a tendency for religious communities to create altars around their own source, their own well. This is natural because everyone experiences the underground river within the context of one's own community, history, mythology, geography, and ritual practices.

The danger lies in thinking of one particular well as the *only* access to the Underground River, and failing to recognize the validity and beauty of other experiences of the Sacred in a vast and diverse world.

HISTORICAL NOTES

While the 13th and 14th centuries were a golden age of apophatic mysticism, its roots emerge as early as the third century. In the sixth century, a theologian, writing under the pseudonym of Dionysius the Areopagite, squarely placed apophatic discourse at the center of Christian thought.

Pseudo-Dionysius, who claimed the guise of a convert of the Apostle Paul,[10] "wrote most specifically of the twin elements of kataphasis (saying) and apophasis (unsaying) in 'mystical theology' (a term Dionysius coined), with the apophatic element being the 'higher' or more accurate."[11]

John Scotus Eriugena in the ninth century drew heavily from Pseudo-Dionysius for his mystical work *Periphyseon* (*On Nature*). A second text that relied extensively on Pseudo-Dionysius was *The Cloud of Unknowing*,[12] whose author is unknown. The text, written in Middle English in the latter half of the 14th century, is replete with apophatic meditation.

Like other apophatic writers in the Middle Ages, the author of *The Cloud of Unknowing* acknowledged it was impossible to think our way into full comprehension of the Divine, but one could fully experience the Divine in the ecstasy of love. In chapter six of *The Cloud of Unknowing*, we read that no person . . .

> . . . can think of God as God's self. Therefore, it is my wish to leave everything that I can think of and choose for my love the thing that I cannot think. Because God can certainly be loved, but not thought. God can be taken and held by love but not by thought. Therefore, though it is good at times to think of the kindness and worthiness of God in particular, and though this is a light and a part of contemplation, nevertheless, in this exercise, it must be cast down and covered over with a cloud of forgetting . . . . You are to smite upon that thick cloud of unknowing with a sharp dart of longing love.[13]

Even though apophatic discourse drew heavily on the understanding of the Divine expressed in the Hebrew Scriptures and Jewish thought, most of its early medieval writers were Christians. By the ninth century, however, some Islamic and Jewish mystics, apophatic thinkers, were circulating writings of unsaying.[14]

Apophasis also appears in mystical texts beyond the boundaries of Western spirituality. Within the Taoist *Tao Te Ching*, the *Vimalakirti Sutra* in Mahayana Buddhism and especially in the language design of Zen *koans*, apophasis uses paradoxical formulas and words of unsaying to articulate experiences of the holy.

Explaining the apophatic nature of the *Vimalakirti Sutra*, Professor Michael Sells writes that it "asserts that 'all constructs are empty' and then playfully turns the statement back upon itself with the assertions that 'the construct that all constructs are empty is empty,' and 'the construct that the construct that all constructs are empty is empty is empty.'"[15]

The "flowering of apophatic mysticism," which occurred during the 150 years from the mid-12th to the beginning of the 14th centuries, saw, almost simultaneously, the emergence of Islamic, Jewish, and Christian masterpieces, including the writings of Ibn al-'Arabi, Jalal al-Din Rumi, Abraham Abulafia, Moses de León, and the Beguine mystics, culminating with Hadewijch of Magdeburg, Marguerite Porete, and Meister Eckhart.[16]

One also can see apophatic traces in other medieval mystics, such as Moses Maimonides, Dante Alighieri, Teresa of Ávila, Julian of Norwich, Jacob Boehme, and Isaac Luria Ashkenazi, to name a few. They are mystics who held to a kind of pan*en*theism (God is present everywhere, in everything, and in everybody), a crucial feature of apophasis.

By the time of the Protestant Reformation, however, apophatic mysticism had moved from the center of medieval Christian mysticism to the margins or underground, thanks in part to the full swing of the Inquisition; but it remained vibrant in Jewish and Sufi traditions.

Apophasis reemerged with force when 20th-century spiritual writers and theologians, many of whom are mentioned in this book or cited in the bibliography, began discussing the impossibility of finding language that fully communicates the Ultimate Reality, the Divine, the Ineffable.

Toward the end of his life, the mystic Teilhard de Chardin wrote, "Humanity is being brought to a moment when it will have to choose between suicide and adoration."[17] He died in the mid-1950's, at a time when people yearned for the simplicity of society and religion to make sense of a post-industrial, post-World War world—an "us and them" world.

For many, chaos and the onslaught of information framing a crumbling world, especially on daily television news, created a need for "clamping down" and rigidity in politics and religion. In a way, fundamentalism and inflexible politics are a suicide of spirit, a giving-in to despair, choosing to escape impending doom or frantically fight it.

Escape is understandable, especially among populations on the margins of power and wealth. However, inflexibility is not the only option. Some take another path and refuse to structure life within a well-prescribed rigidity, choosing instead adoration, a particular kind of adoration that scholars and theologians call apophatic mysticism.

CHARACTERISTICS

Mysticism Generally

It is important to map out some of the definitions, distinctions, and character-istics of mysticism. William James' well-received *The Varieties of Religious Experience* outlines four characteristics, which still resonate a century later, to which scholars have added a few others:

1. Ineffability (inability to capture the experience in ordinary language)

Something "ineffable" is beyond the descriptive power of words. The Aurora Borealis phenomenon described in Sid's story, for example, may have a scientific explanation; but a teenager trying to describe a Northern Lights experience to his grandmother is another matter altogether. Feeling "con-nected to everything, connected to God"? What does that even mean?

2. Noetic Quality (the notion that mystical experiences reveal an otherwise hidden or inaccessible knowledge)

Authentic mystical encounters are noetic; there is an understanding that what has been experienced is beyond the ordinary, something that one can intuit intellectually, an "inner knowing," yet beyond explanation. Since explana-tions are always inadequate in unfolding the mystical experience, there is the sense that trying to elucidate intuitive understanding through rational expla-nation somehow reduces it to less than its sum and actually diminishes Di-vinity itself. Some spiritual cultures discourage trying to explain a mystical encounter for that reason.

After having just walked on the moon, Apollo 14 astronaut Edgar Mitch-ell had an experience that transformed his life. As he was returning to the planet he knew as home, an inner conviction filled him that the beautiful blue world at which he gazed is part of a living system, harmonious and whole; and, as he expressed it later, we all participate "in a universe of conscious-ness."[18] His worldview changed in an instant. Mitchell had felt the depth of human consciousness in his own mystical union with planet Earth.

When Sid shared his Northern Lights experience with his grandmother, he tried to convey this feeling of oneness, the sense that the division of God and humanity, or the heavens and earth, had dissolved. He described this as "the feeling of being connected to everything in the universe, of being con-nected with God." But, even as he expressed this, language failed him. When she replied, "Aren't the Northern Lights beautiful?" he knew it was not just the stars and sky that were lovely—it was the feeling of oneness, wholeness, and completeness he felt in their cosmic dance.

3. Transiency (mystical experiences last for relatively brief periods)

The next two characteristics of mysticism identified by William James are "less sharply marked, but . . . usually found."[19]

Mystical states do not sustain themselves for long. A half an hour, or at most an hour or two, seems to be "the limit beyond which they fade into the light of common day,"[20] although typically they are much briefer.

4. Passivity (the sense that mystical experiences are beyond human volition and control)

Many mystics and mysticism writers discuss disciplines for attaining mystical union, certain practices that can open the way for the ineffable encounter. However, most agree that these are merely preparation, ways of being awake to something over which one has no control. In that sense, mystical experiences simply happen to us, whether solicited or not.

James describes passivity this way: "Although the oncoming of mystical states may be facilitated by preliminary voluntary operations, as by fixing the attention, or going through certain bodily performances, or in other ways which manuals of mysticism prescribe; yet when the characteristic sort of consciousness once has set in, the mystic feels as if his own will were in abeyance, and indeed sometimes as if he were grasped and held by a superior power."[21]

5. Unity of opposites (a sense of Oneness, Wholeness or Completeness)

In addition to the four characteristics that James identified, F. C. Happold's classic *Mysticism* puts forth another three.[22] The first is unity of opposites: "A common characteristic of many mystical states is the presence of a consciousness of the Oneness of everything . . . . In mystical experience the dilemma of duality is resolved. For to the mystic is given that unifying vision of the One in the All and the All in the One."[23]

The experience of sweet mystical communion often results in the unity of opposites, or, better, what we perceive to be opposites. Many spiritual authors try to articulate this sense of oneness and dissolving of duality—the bridging of opposites, whether immanent and transcendent, feminine and masculine, soul and body, or mystical union and justice-making. As Jalal ad-Din Rumi put it in his typically pithy, but insightful, way, "Out beyond ideas of wrongdoing and rightdoing, there is a field; I will meet you there."[24]

6. Timelessness (a sense that mystical experiences transcend time)

Mystical experiences seem to occur beyond time, and, in some sense, outside time. They may even rebuff time and space as illusory. Like the mystical unity of opposites, timelessness has paradoxical elements.

For Happold, ". . . the experiences of the mystics are not understandable unless one is prepared to accept that there may be an entirely different dimension from that of clock time or indeed of any other sort of time. For the mystic feels himself to be in a dimension where time is not, where 'all is always now.'"[25]

People, who have a mystical encounter, sense they are in the here and now, given completely over into the present moment. They can be listening to a stirring musical performance, watching a baby's first steps, engaged in thoughtful conversation, attending a brilliant speech, or viewing a spectacular evening sky lightshow from a Lake Michigan dock; and the immediate rapture of the moment transports them into a different place.

Some individuals have described themselves as "being caught up" (like the Apostle Paul) for a period of time—three minutes, five minutes, or ten; but most recognize that, even if the experience lasts a split second, time was transposed into eternity.

On his own timelessness experience, philosophy professor Douglas Shrader reports it "can be separated into two discrete temporal segments. As I struggled to make sense of the experience, sorting through my conceptual toolbox and linguistic dictionary, there was an altered but nonetheless recognizable sense of duration and temporal succession (before/after). Upon surrender, those familiar temporal parameters dissolved so completely as to leave no trace."[26]

7. A feeling that one has somehow encountered "the true self" (a sense that mystical experiences reveal the nature of our true, cosmic self: one beyond life and death, beyond difference and duality, and beyond ego and selfishness)

Happold writes that, for the mystic, ". . . there is another self, the true Self, which is not affected by ordinary happenings and which gives . . . a sense of identity through numerous bodily and mental transformations. It does not change in the slow changes of the organism, in the flux of sensations, in the dissipation of ideas, or in the fading of memories."[27]

All mystical traditions reflect Happold's theory. Hinduism articulates this notion as the merger of the *atman* (the individual self) and the *Brahman* (the universal self). For Buddhists, "the goal is the transpersonal awakening to boundless awareness, non-dual experience, and infinite compassion."[28]

Because of this transformation of ego-self into true-self, individuals, who experience mystical union, often feel it is propelled by forces beyond their control into new directions that require authenticity and witnessing, as such, to the experience that enveloped them (seeing themselves in a whole different light).

Core Tenets of Apophatic Mysticism

1. *Divinity as No-thing*

Apophatic mysticism asserts that Divinity, "God," Ultimate Reality, or however one names the ineffable, is essentially unnamable. To name Divinity is to carve it into a graven image, to reduce it to an object, which inherently contradicts the notion of Divinity being beyond objectification.

However, the mystic also recognizes that the limits of language require us to call that which is beyond objectifying an "it" for purposes of communicating this mystery with each other. There is an underlying paradox when trying to express an understanding of the Divine through words. This leads to a unique form of dialog, the dialog of "unsaying." Starhawk captures this beautifully in her "Prayer for the Ground of Being": "Nameless One—of many Names."[29]

Sufis recognize that "the names—the words *we use and refer to* as divine names—are not the Names (as God would "know" them) but merely the 'names of the Name' . . . revealed through the Qur'an and the hadith to those who intimately are connected to God."[30]

Similarly, Meister Eckhart writes, "God is nothing. No thing. God is nothingness; and yet God is something. God is neither this thing nor that thing that we can express. God, a being beyond all being, is a beingless being."[31]

2. *Emphasis on Letting Go*

Another apophasis component is the idea that Divinity is not something to be contained, captured, yoked to, or "saved" toward. Most medieval apophatic mystics, regardless of their tradition, believed that spirituality is a matter of subtraction, not addition.

Traditional Western thought, particularly in Judaism and Christianity, holds that, since Adam's disobedience, humans are out of communion with God. Apophatic mystics, however, tend to believe that we are all already in communion with the Divine, but most of us are simply unaware of this union or cast it aside. Hence, the ". . . goal of the mystic is not to achieve *unity* with God but rather to achieve full transcognitive *awareness* of *already* being one with the One."[32] Rumi gets at this when he quips, "Can you find another market like this? Where, with your one rose, you can buy hundreds of rose gardens?"

Similar to the Buddhist idea of awakening, apophatic mystics recognize that the fullness of Divinity is already present in every aspect of creation, including humanity. For them, Adam's act of disobedience did not lead to a fall from grace, but a fall from the realization of grace. That which separates us from God is not Original Sin, pride, or shame, but the trappings of worldliness, materialism, misuse of power, and so on. Thus, spirituality is not adding on something to achieve union with God, but letting go, and letting be. Paul Tillich calls this "an experience which has a paradoxical character, the character of accepting acceptance."[33]

Common apophatic images for expressing communion with the Divine include words like "awakening," "letting go," "being lost," "emptying," "flowing out," and "sinking." Once the mystic has let go and sunk into nothingness, out of that nothing, Divinity "breaks through," "bursts forth," "is birthed," or is described like "a spark," "light," or "shining."

3. Failure of Language and Symbol

Since Divinity is ineffable and one can only "see God's back," as Moses' encounter with God on Mount Sinai is expressed, apophatic mysticism holds two general principles about language. The first is that any "saying" of, or about, God needs to be "unsaid" in a process of regression.

The second principle is in the tendency to interrupt the practice by using capital letters for words related to Divinity. Since a core element of apophatic mysticism is the idea that God is beyond any name for God, many mystics are uncomfortable with capitalizing divine names since it subtly suggests one's own construct of God is *God*, which it is not. As Eckhart writes, "Why I pray God to rid me of God is because conditionless being is above God and above distinction."[34]

4. Panentheistic

Panentheism is another characteristic common to apophatic mystics. It is the idea that Divinity is in all things, and all things contain the fullness of Divinity, yet Divinity is beyond the sum of all things. This holds in paradoxical tension the immanent and transcendent natures of Divinity while resisting the temptation to frame these natures as separate or dualistic.

Most American Indian spiritualities reflect this understanding with the Great Spirit—a being beyond being—which is in and through all things, but encompassing each of those things.

Since Divinity is found everywhere or, as Eckhart states, "Every creature is a Word of God," apophatic mystics embrace mystery as a referential openness. In other words, they have openness to the depths of their tradition, if they have one, and are in conversation with other traditions. This openness sometimes leads to mainline theological condemnations of apophatic mystics as heretical.

5. Revealed in the Common

Apophatic mysticism yearns and strives toward being awake to the Divine, but it also recognizes that its ultimate aim is a spirituality lived in the world. It is not just about the mystic herself or himself, but about all creation. In that sense, apophatic mysticism is worldly. There is, of course, a place for solitude and exploring one's inner depths, and even temporary asceticism, such as fasting; but these are points on the pathway toward an awakening of the New Creation, which includes everything God has made and is making.

Eckhart is most explicit in countering the notion of mysticism as something extraordinary and removed from everyday reality. For him, the noblest and most extraordinary of all events (the birth of the divine Son in the soul) is the most common (any act of justice, insofar as it is just)."[35]

6. Service to the Community

Most mystics steadfastly believe that part and parcel of emptying ourselves to receive the Divine or being in union with the Divine is the giving of ourselves to others through altruism and works of justice, which we sometimes call, appropriately enough, self-sacrifice. Rumi referred to himself as a "slave" in carrying out deeds of service with the joy of worship.

A personal example from one of the authors is Jim's grandmother who was devoutly spiritual during her 93 years of life. She lived simply, gave her money to the poor, walked to church every day, greeted everyone on the street, was the secret Santa for her six grandchildren, and helped put them through Catholic school. She did not drive, but would walk miles to visit someone in the hospital or nursing home. She attended funerals for old people who had died alone so that "someone would be there to say 'goodbye' and pray for them." And, at age 82, she walked the United Farm Workers grape boycott picket line in front of a local grocery store.

Jim's grandmother "walked the talk" of the Gospel of love and justice in which she found God, and God found her. When she died, all kinds of people, unknown to the family, came to the funeral home and church. They were people whose lives she had gently touched and whom she would have prayed that God touched through her.

7. Interspirituality

Wayne Teasdale, the monk and proponent of interfaith dialog, expressed the universal and foundational quality of mysticism as interspirituality: "Interspirituality points to the realization that although there are many spiritual paths, a universal commonality underlies them all . . . . The real religion of humankind can be said to be spirituality itself, because mystical spirituality is the origin of all the world religions."[36]

Although referring to other Christian denominations, 18th-century cleric John Wesley's words ring true in a broader interfaith context:

> But even though a difference in opinions or modes of worship may prevent an entire external union, yet need it prevent our union in affection? Though we cannot think alike, may we not love alike? May we not be of one heart, though we are not of one opinion? Without doubt, we may. In this all the children of God may unite, even though they retain these smaller differences. These remaining as they are, they may help one another increase in love and in good works. [37]

Advocates of interspirituality understand that multiple wells access the Underground River and that we can learn much from each another in our various traditions. However, it is also important to distinguish that language and cultural nuances can lead to very different things in spirituality. We cannot assume we are speaking of the same concepts, even if using similar language. The aim of mystical union differs greatly, depending on the setting. Many people focus their spiritual life on a personal God or "Great Spirit." However, not all Western mysticism is "object-centered," particularly within the apophatic tradition where union with the Divine focuses on the supreme *subject*.

Interspirituality seeks to recognize the beauty and dignity of other traditions besides one's own, to hear the rumbling of the River below, a river that connects and validates all authentic mystical experience.

One appeal of New Age spiritualities is their creative syncretistic ability to hold on to the attractive aspects of one's own tradition, while borrowing freely from other religions, pop psychology, and other current trends.

Interspirituality, however, is not a blend-all-mystical-experiences-together that minimizes or "flattens" the fullness represented in a tradition. Interspirituality is not about eliminating the world's rich diversity of religious expression or rejecting these traditions' individuality for a homogenous super-spirituality. It is not an effort to create a new form of spiritual culture. Instead, it is an attempt to make available to everyone all the insight from others that the spiritual journey assumes and needs. [38]

Nor is it the goal of interspirituality to encourage jumping from one tradition to another, believing somehow that another tradition has more to offer than the spiritual path of one's origin. Sometimes, though, one's own spiritual background carries so much baggage that one must leave the path of origin and trek along a new path to be liberated into spiritual wholeness or find authentic mystical union.

In many cases, when one does the hard task of excavating the richness of one's own tradition, the realization eventually emerges that we are all drinking from the same underground river, though from different wells.

Mysticism that embraces interspirituality allows the opportunity to explore the deeper rhythms of one's own spiritual tradition while honoring the wealth that comes from other traditions. Sometimes seeing something practiced in a mythological and ritual context outside our own tradition allows us to see afresh aspects of our tradition that may have remained hidden. The recognition that religions are a syncretistic blend from multiple influences also frees us to risk incorporating elements from other traditions we might otherwise have overlooked.

DANGERS OF MYSTICISM

It is important to mention briefly the dangers of mysticism. The Book of Common Prayer has an admonishment in the wedding ceremony that marriage "is not by any to be entered into unadvisedly or lightly; but reverently, discreetly, advisedly, soberly, and in the fear of God." The same can be said of mysticism.

Three recurring dangers are evident across traditions. The paradox of desire coupled with the ultimate inability to comprehend the ineffability of the Divine, especially for the unprepared practitioner, can lead to "madness." Celts describe this as being stuck within the thin veil.

Another liability comes from the inability to distinguish oneself from the Divine, an enmeshment of sorts in the ecstatic experience. This leads to the sense that one has a special and unique relationship with the Divine; and, unless others experience divinity in that same way, they are somehow less— less enlightened or diminished—what classic theologians call "apostasy."

The third threat occurs when a mystic cannot see herself or himself as separate from the ineffable, or divine. To use the concept in Jewish tradition, it is the inability to differentiate between the "i" of *ego* and the "I"—*I Amness* of that which is beyond definition or language. This last danger is commonly called "heresy,"[39] when the mystic sees herself or himself as God.

These common dangers arise in various forms within the mystical traditions of Judaism, Islam, and Christianity—a reminder that one must approach the mystical pathway with respect and conscious awareness, and preferably with an experienced spiritual guide.

Hopefully, this overview will help make it a bit easier to follow the dialog of Jalal ad-Din Rumi, Moses de León, and Meister Eckhart later in this book.

NOTES

1. Matthew Fox, *The Coming of the Cosmic Christ: The Healing of Mother Earth and the Birth of a Global Renaissance* (San Francisco: Harper & Row, 1988), 38–40.

2. Douglas W. Shrader, "Seven Characteristics of Mystical Experiences," *Annual Hawaii International Conference on Arts and Humanities* (2008), 3, at http://www.oneonta.edu/aca-

demics/philos/shrader/MysticalExperiences.pdf ("Etymologically speaking, a mystic is a person who has been initiated into secret rites (Latin *mysticus*, from Greek *mustikos*, from *mustes*).").

3. Michael A. Sells, *Mystical Languages of Unsaying* (Chicago: University of Chicago, 1994), 2.

4. Ori Z. Soltes, *Mysticism in Judaism, Christianity, and Islam: Searching for Oneness* (Lanham, MD: Rowman & Littlefield, 2009), 94.

5. Marion Zimmer Bradley, *The Mists of Avalon* (New York: Random House, 1982.

6. Fox, *The Coming of the Cosmic Christ*, 38–40.

7. Evelyn Underhill, "The Characteristics of Mysticism, 1911" (vol. IV, 72), *Sacred Texts*, http://www.sacred-texts.com/myst/myst/myst07.htm.

8. Mircea Eliade, *Myths, Dreams, and Mysteries: The Encounter Between Contemporary Faiths and Archaic Realities*, trans. Philip Mairet (New York: Harper & Row, 1975), 23.

9. Mircea Eliade, *The Sacred and the Profane: The Nature of Religion*, trans. Willard R. Trask (New York: Harcourt, Brace & World, Inc., 1957), 72; and, PDF text, at https://www.dmt-nexus.me/doc/the%20sacred%20and%20the%20profane.pdf.

10. Pseudo-Dionysius the Areopagite was a Christian theologian, philosopher, and mystic of the late 5th to early 6th centuries and author of the *Corpus Areopagiticum* (or *Corpus Dionysiacum*). The author pseudonymously identified himself as the Athenian convert of Paul mentioned in the Acts of the Apostles (17:34). This false attribution gave his work authority in theological writing. In recent years, interest has focused again on the book because of its influence in Christian thought, as well as modern repudiation of older criticism that it was fundamentally Neoplatonic, and therefore non-Christian, theology, and because of interest in parallels between modern linguistic theory and Dionysius' reflections on language and negative theology ("unsaying").

11. Sells, *Mystical Languages of Unsaying*, 5, 8–9.

12. *The Cloud of Unknowing*, ed. Evelyn Underhill (1922), PDF text, http://sacred-texts.com/chr/cou/index.htm .

13. Ibid., at http://sacred-texts.com/chr/cou/cou11.htm.

14. Sells, *Mystical Languages of Unsaying*, 5.

15. Ibid., 4.

16. Ibid.

17. *The Essential Mystics: The Soul's Journey into Truth*, ed. Andrew Harvey (San Francisco: HarperSanFrancisco, 1996), xv.

18. Linda Sechrist, "Exploring the Last Frontier with Astronaut Edgar Mitchell," *Natural Awakenings*, Dec. 2011, http://www.naturalawakeningsmag.com/Natural-Awakenings/December-2011/Exploring-the-Last-Frontier-with-Astronaut-Edgar-Mitchell/.

19. William James, *The Varieties of Religious Experience: A Study in Human Nature* (New York: New American Library of World Literature, Inc., 1958), 416.

20. Ibid.

21. Ibid.

22. F. C. Happold, *Mysticism* (New York: Penguin Books, 1970), 93.

23. Ibid., 46–47.

24. David Wilcox and Nancy Pettit, *Out Beyond Ideas*, 2014, http://www.outbey ondideas.org/.

25. Ibid., 48.

26. Shrader, "Seven Characteristics of Mystical Experiences," 14.

27. Happold, *Mysticism*, 48.

28. Wayne Teasdale, *The Mystic Heart: Discovering a Universal Spirituality in the World's Religions* (Novato, CA: New World Library, 2001), 25.

29. Starhawk, *Starhawk's Tangled Web*, http://www.starhawk.org/.

30. Soltes, *Mysticism in Judaism, Christianity, and Islam*, 96.

31. Matthew Fox, *Meditations with Meister Eckhart* (Rochester, VT: Bear & Company, 1983), 41.

32. Soltes, *Mysticism in Judaism, Christianity, and Islam*, 98.

33. Paul Tillich, *The Courage To Be* (Binghamton, NY: Vail-Ballou Press, 1979), 172.

34. This is one of those widely-cited, widely-accepted quotations that appear occasionally in this book, attributed to either Meister Eckhart or Rumi, without noting the source, but wholly consistent with that mystic's thought. See, e.g., "Introduction to Meister Eckhart," http://www.esoteric.msu.edu/REL275/EckhartIntroduction.html.

35. Sells, *Mystical Languages of Unsaying*, 7–8.

36. Wayne Teasdale, *The Mystic Hours: A Daybook of Inspirational Wisdom and Devotion* (Novato, CA: New World Library, 2004), 26.

37. John Wesley, *The Works of John Wesley* (Grand Rapids, MI: Baker Book House, 1978) (vol. I, Sermon XXXIX, "Catholic Spirit, No. 4").

38. Teasdale, *The Mystic Hours*, 26.

39. Soltes, *Mysticism in Judaism, Christianity, and Islam*, 95.

Chapter Four

The 13th and Early 14th Centuries as Backdrop

People should not pride themselves for loving their own country,
but rather for loving the whole world.
The earth is but one country; and humankind, its citizens.

—Baha'u'llah

The lives of Jalal ad-Din Rumi (Mevlana, "Master," as the non-Western world commonly knows him), Meister Eckhart, and Moses de León stretched a century and a quarter from 1207 to 1327. They inhabited three different areas in the world, each with its own distinct culture and history. Much happened during that remarkable period when they walked the earth and gave enormous impetus to the rise and flowering of apophatic mysticism.

Great contradictions and countervailing impulses filled those 125 years that swirled around them. There were bloody wars and gruesome conquests, chaotic events, and incredible advances in science, culture, and knowledge, albeit uneven. It was a period of isolating tendencies, but also of brilliant creativities; and a time that produced some of the brightest legal and spiritual minds.

Centuries, as time markers, of course, are arbitrary constructs, subjective demarcations to help humans get some kind of grasp on history's march. The 13th century is generally considered the third, and last, century of the "High Middle Ages," although that era does stretch a bit into the 14th century.

Thirteenth-century Europe underwent astonishing social and political change. In addition, the rapid development of coal as an energy source, which began in Newcastle, England in 1232, and a sharp population increase across the continent helped propel the economy. By mid-century, prosperity reached levels that would not happen again in some regions until the 19th century.

A succession of natural and human-made calamities in the 14th century (Late Middle Ages), however, reversed or undermined the advances, culminating at the end of the preceding century, with disastrous economic and social consequences. Most notable were the "little ice age" and famine, the Black Death (the pandemic plague that took the lives of some 25 million people in Europe alone from 1347–1351), numerous wars (such as the Hundred Years War that began in 1337), and breakdown of social structures.

Overall, by the end of the High Middle Ages great intellectual, spiritual, and artistic endeavors had developed and expanded; and the growth of nationalism in many European states, often based on ethnic identity, had taken hold. During the same period, the powerful Italian city-states began to emerge; and Muslim society in the al-Ándalus region of the Iberian Peninsula shrank rapidly in the face of *reconquista* successes by the Christian kingdoms.

CHRISTIANITY IN EUROPE

After the Great Schism between the Western and Eastern churches in 1054, the Eastern (Byzantine) imperial church in Constantinople continued to assert universal authority. By the 13th century, however, this claim became increasingly irrelevant as the Eastern Roman Empire shrank, and the Ottoman Turks conquered most of what was left of the Byzantine Empire (indirectly aided by the Crusades and invasions from the West). The other Eastern churches in communion with Constantinople were not part of that empire and increasingly acted independently, only nominally recognizing Constantinople's hierarchical role.

After Mongol rule began in Russia in the 1220s and lasted into the 15th century, the Russian Church enjoyed a favored position, obtaining immunity from taxation, and eventually establishing itself as the protector of Orthodoxy.

In Western Europe, the Holy Roman Empire fragmented, making it less of an empire as well; and the Roman Church struggled to assert unity and supremacy.

New mendicant religious orders appeared. Francis of Assisi, himself a prominent mystic, founded the Franciscans in 1209; and Dominic de Guzmán of Old Castile established the Dominicans in 1215. They were called mendicant orders (from the Latin "to beg") because their members took a vow of poverty, individually and collectively, and lived from what people donated to them, following the example of Jesus by traveling, preaching, teaching, and doing works of mercy.

The earlier-founded monastic religious orders, especially the Benedictines, Cistercians, and Premonstratensians, continued to perform an important role in reforming Christianity and advancing scholarship throughout the 13th century, as did two earlier mendicant orders, the Augustinians and Carmelites.

Pope Gregory IX initiated the Medieval Inquisition in 1231, assigning the Dominicans the responsibility of combating heresy. In 1252, torture became an official instrument of the Inquisition. The Medieval Inquisition reached its apex in the second half of the 13th century, although other Inquisitions followed later, most notably in Spain and Portugal.

In 1272–1274, the Second Council of Lyons attempted to unite the Churches of the Eastern Roman Empire and the Church of Rome, but failed.

There was a flourishing of mystical theology in the latter part of the 13th century, right before Meister Eckhart came onto the scene, in which women such as Mechthild of Magdeburg, Mechthild of Hackeborn, and Gertrude the Great were prominent.

Mechthild of Magdeburg authored *The Flowing Light of the Godhead.* Her criticism of church dignitaries, religious laxity, and claims to theological insight aroused so much opposition that some called for burning her writings. With advancing age, she was alone, and became blind. The Cistercian nuns of Helfta took her in—a courageous act. The nuns were highly educated; Mechthild of Hackeborn and Gertrude the Great lived in that convent as well so that, for some years, the three were in the same place.

Mechthild of Magdeburg was a Beguine. The Beguines (women) and the Beghards (men) were Christian lay religious orders, active in Northern Europe, beginning in the 13th century. Their members lived in semi-monastic communities, but did not take formal religious vows; they were free to leave at any time. They were part of a larger spiritual revival of the era that stressed imitation of Christ's life through voluntary poverty, care of the poor and sick, and religious devotion. They often met fierce opposition from church authorities, who sometimes persecuted them. In a sense, the Beguines were a kind of medieval feminist movement, which would make them even more troublesome for the established order.

Gerard Groote, formerly a successful educator who had had a religious experience and preached a life of simple devotion to Jesus Christ, founded a similar movement, the Brethren of the Common Life, in the Netherlands in mid-14th century. The majority of the Brethren were laymen and did not take monastic vows; there were some women ("sisters"), too. They devoted themselves to charitable deeds, nursing the sick, studying and teaching the Scriptures, and copying spiritual writings. They founded schools renowned for their high learning standards, which many famous men attended, including Nicholas of Cusa, Thomas á Kempis, Erasmus, and Martin Luther.

The movement spread into western and southern Germany and is credited in part with eventually helping to soften the ground for the Protestant Reformation.

The Avignon Papacy began in 1309 and lasted until 1378, during which time the pope lived in France under the king's tutelage. This eventually evolved into the Western Schism (1378–1417) with rival popes in Rome and Avignon.

At Avignon, the moral laxity of church leaders sunk to an all-time low. Petrarch called Avignon "the Babylon of the West." The existence of parallel papacies was more than a power struggle; it was a fundamental challenge to the medieval worldview. The corruption and machinations at Avignon also awakened the earliest stirrings for the Protestant Reformation. The Englishman John Wycliffe and the Bohemian Jan Hus were the first of the reformers.

Catherine of Siena, herself a mystic and a fiercely determined woman, helped engineer an end to this bizarre scandal and returned a unified papacy to Rome.

The Crusades

The Crusades, a series of military campaigns, initially sanctioned by various popes, began at the end of 11th century and lasted into the latter part of the thirteenth. The purposes of the Crusades were as mixed as the goals of their leaders. For some, it was a war against Islamic expansion; for others, it was part of long-running struggle over European hegemony. And, for some, it was a papal-led enlargement of the Latin Church. The most commonly known Crusades were those that had the stated objective, at least nominally, of restoring Christian access to, and possession of, the religious sites at Jerusalem and the Holy Land generally.

The Crusaders often pillaged the lands through which they marched. The Fourth Crusade was particularly catastrophic. In 1204, after a six-month siege, Crusaders sacked Constantinople and the Church of Holy Wisdom (Hagia Sophia), raped and murdered the inhabitants, confiscated religious relics and conveyed them to locations like Venice, destroyed the Monastery of Stoudios and the Library of Constantinople, and installed the Latin Empire there. That saga of atrocities doomed any hope of reuniting the East and West Christian Churches, and led to the weakening and eventual fall of the Byzantine Empire to the Ottomans.[1]

The politics of the Crusades were complicated, contradictory, and sometimes Machiavellian, even to the point of conspiracies leading to alliances between combatants of different faiths against coreligionists. The Crusades culminated in failure in 1291 with the fall of the last Christian fortress at Acre, capital of the Crusader Kingdom of Jerusalem, to Muslim forces.

The Crusades left an enormous nick on history, both awful and awesome. Independent states came into existence. Europe reached out overseas, reopening the Mediterranean to trade and travel, thus enabling Genoa and Venice to flourish. The marching armies would do business with the local populations, and Byzantine emperors often organized markets for them as they traveled through their territory. The crusading movement consolidated the collective identity of the Latin Church under the pope's leadership and was a source of heroism, chivalry, and medieval piety. This, in turn, spawned medieval romance, philosophy, and literature. The Robin Hood ballad emerged during this time, as did expansion of the Holy Grail legend.

The Crusades reinforced the symbiosis of Western Christendom, feudalism, and militarism. The fierce preaching by Pope Urban II for the First Crusade touched off the Rhineland massacres of thousands of Jews, an event that Jewish leaders in the 19th century used to support Zionism.

THE MONGOLS

The first quarter of the 13th century also saw the rise of Genghis Khan in Mongolia, who eventually expanded his empire to include much of Northern China, Korea, and the Persian Empire and reached the Russian Steppes, due largely to brilliant tactical uses of horse archers. They were fierce and fearful warriors, often massacring those in their way.

His son, "the Great Khan," continued the project of conquest, subduing northern China and ravaging much of Eastern Europe. But the Mongol advance on the Muslim world was blocked at the Battle of Ain Jalut, near Nazareth (1260), where the Mamluk rulers of Egypt carried the day.

Under Kublai Khan, the grandson of Genghis Khan, the Mongol empire became second in size only to the British Empire, which came centuries later. But it was first in contiguous land mass, controlling about a fifth of the world's geography and a quarter of its population. By the time of Kublai's death in 1294, however, the empire had fractured into four separate khanates.

In the last quarter of the 13th century, young Marco Polo, led by his father and uncle, set off for China, where they apparently met Kublai Khan. He returned to Venice twenty-four years later after traveling 15,000 miles through Asia, Persia, China, and Indonesia. The *Book of the Marvels of the World* (*The Travels of Marco Polo*), a travelogue of stories, was a popular sensation in Europe, even before the printing press, and inspired Christopher Columbus and other explorers. It also influenced European cartography, eventually leading to the Fra Mauro map. But, interestingly, people did not believe Marco Polo when he reported that the Chinese used paper money.

Pax Mongolica

After establishing their rule, the Mongols relaxed their fierceness of battle and showed relative openness to foreigners. This led to a remarkably broad cultural exchange of peoples, products, technology, and science.[2]

The Mongols expedited and encouraged travel, permitting European merchants, craftsmen, and envoys to travel to China for the first time. Their empire linked Europe and Asia, and ushered in an era of extended contacts between East and West. Sought-after valuable Asian goods reached Europe along the caravan trails (earlier named the "Silk Roads"), which eventually inspired the search for a sea route to Asia.

The Mongols were tolerant toward religions other than their own or at least had an attitude of benign neglect. Even though they generally practiced shamanism, the Mongols decided early on that forcefully imposing their religion would be counter-productive. Instead, they cultivated Buddhist, Muslim, and Christian clerics in newly conquered lands to win their support and offered them tax benefits.

The Mongols' relation with Islam had tremendous impact on their associations with other peoples. They enlisted Muslims to help rule China, especially as financial administrators, because they did not trust the Chinese. They also recognized Islamic scholars' advancements in astronomy and medicine and recruited many of them to China.

The Khans' architectural projects and construction of networks of roads and postal stations throughout the realm promoted developments in science and engineering.

The later Mongol era patronized painting and theater. They engaged Confucian scholars and Tibetan Buddhist monks as advisers, which led to innovative ideas and construction of new temples and monasteries and, in turn, influenced Persian painting.

CULTURE, EDUCATION, AND LAW

European

King Phillip II of France began the 13th century by extending special protection to the University of Paris in the same year it received foundational status (1200). The university offered a traditional liberal education (arts, medicine, law, and theology). Of the other twenty or so medieval universities at the time, the major ones were Bologna (founded 1088), Oxford (founded 1167, chartered 1254), Salamanca (founded 1134, chartered 1254), Cambridge (founded 1209), and Padua (founded 1222).

Ramon Llull, a Majorcan writer, philosopher, and logician in the 13th and early 14th centuries, is credited with the first major work of Catalan literature. A Christian, he tried to convert Muslims and Jews through debate and logic, instead of force. He eventually died at age 82 after being stoned by Muslims near Tunis. His persistent advocacy of linguistic education bore fruit in 1311 when the Council of Vienne ordered the creation of chairs of Hebrew, Arabic, and Chaldean (Aramaic) at the Universities of Bologna, Oxford, Paris, and Salamanca.

Also in the 13th century, the motet form began to develop out of the *ars antiqua* tradition of Western European music. Cimabue, the Florentine painter, lived in the same era, as did Andrea of Grosseto, an Italian poet and writer, often considered to be the first author in the Italian language, and Snorri Sturluson, Icelandic historian and saga-writer.

The first quarter of the 14th century was the beginning of the Italian Renaissance with writers like Dante Durante degli Alighieri, Petrarch, and Boccaccio (known collectively as "the three fountains" or "the three crowns"), and painters like Giotto.

Dante was an Italian poet, prose writer, literary theorist, moral philosopher, and political thinker—and also probably a mystic. His monumental epic *La Commedia*, later named *La Divina Commedia* (*Divine Comedy*) by Boccaccio, is thought to be the greatest literary writing in Italian, and a masterpiece of world literature. In Italy, he is known as "il Sommo Poeta" ("the Supreme Poet") or just "il Poeta," and considered the "Father of the Italian language."

Architecture saw a transition from Romanesque to Gothic styles; many notable Gothic cathedrals were built or completed during this era, the Chartres cathedral (1260) being an iconic example.

As to law, in the 13th century, a judicial metamorphosis took place across Europe. Irrational trial standards and practices (such as trial by ordeal) gave way to evidence-driven jurisprudential systems that still operate to this day, albeit in much more refined form.

Islamic Spain

In the entire Western world, culture and education was most vigorous and thriving for half a millennium during the High Middle Ages in what is modern-day Spain. Jewish and Islamic culture, science, and thought gave rise to a "golden age" in al-Ándalus, as the Moorish region was then called, which stretched from east to west and covered the southern two-thirds of the Iberian Peninsula. This ended with the Christian kings' persecution and expulsion of Jews and Muslims from the region at the end of the 15th century.[3]

Though Muslims governed the region, they afforded Jews and Christians protected status, a modus vivendi, something less than full citizenship, but far better than the treatment accorded Jews and Muslims in Christian countries.

Al-Ándalus was in frequent battle with the Catholic kingdoms to the north and west; a significant number of its residents converted to Islam. The Homeric-like epic *El Cantar de Myo Çid* (*The Song of My Cid*), which emerged around the turn of 1300, reflects these tensions and realities.

The Moors had arrived on the peninsula in 711, and eventually built magnificent cities like Granada (home to the exquisite Alhambra Palace), Toledo, Córdoba, Seville, and Cádiz.

Córdoba, the governing city of the region by the 10th century, was much like a modern metropolis—graceful architecture, paved streets, raised pedestrian sidewalks, and "downtown" lighted pathways at night. This was several hundred years before there was a paved street in Paris or a street lamp in London.

Córdoba had more than a million residents, 200,000 homes, 800 public schools, a variety of colleges and universities, palaces surrounded by beautiful gardens, thousands of public markets and mills, and hundreds of public baths (at a time when cleanliness in Christian Europe was not yet a virtue).

The Great Mosque of Córdoba (La Mezquita) is still one of the architectural wonders of the world despite later inelegant and crude Spanish alterations. Thousands of brass and silver lamps, which burned perfumed oil, lit its low gold and scarlet roof, supported by 1,200 columns of marble, jasper, and porphyry (of which 850 remain).

Al-Ándalus' tanneries were among the best. Copper, gold, tin, silver, lead, iron, quicksilver, and alum were mined extensively. Toledo's sword blades were unsurpassed in Europe, and Murcia's factories produced fine brass and iron instruments.

Education was universal in Moorish Spain, while most of Christian Europe was illiterate—not even the kings and lords could read or write. There were more than seventeen well-respected universities in the Moorish region. In fact, in the 10th and 11th centuries, some seventy public libraries were established; none existed in Christian Europe. The Córdoba library itself held more than 600,000 manuscripts.

Scientific progress in astronomy, chemistry, geography, mathematics, physics, philosophy, and intellectual life as a whole thrived. Scholars, artists, and scientists formed learning societies, and organized congresses to promote research and facilitate the spread of knowledge. Córdoba became one of the world's leading centers of medicine and philosophical debate.

Islamic scholars explored the early Greek philosophers, such as Plato, Plotinus, and Aristotle. Indeed, because of their writings and their Latin translations of old texts that had been preserved, they effectively re-introduced these philosophers to Europe.

The premier al-Ándalus philosopher Averroës (Ibn Rushd) (1126–1198) of Córdoba founded the 13th-century philosophical movement that became known as Averroism. His labors led to the popularization of Aristotle and were responsible for the development of Scholasticism in medieval Europe.

Averroës was a prototypical Muslim "Renaissance Man," a true master of Aristotelian philosophy, Islamic philosophy and theology, Maliki (Sunni) jurisprudence, logic, psychology, politics, and Andalusian classical music theory. He was skilled in medicine, astronomy, geography, mathematics, physics, and celestial mechanics.

Averroës had to defend Aristotelian philosophy against dogmatic Islamic theologians, and was controversial in Muslim circles, where he had little influence. Nor did he have any discernible impact on Islamic philosophic thought until modern times. His *Fasl al-Maqāl* (The Decisive Treatise) stresses the importance of analytical thinking as a prerequisite to interpreting the Qur'an. He had greater impact on Western Europe and has been called its "founding father of secular thought."

Averroës is most renowned for his Arabic commentaries on Aristotle's writings, which had been mostly forgotten in the West. Before 1150, only a few of Aristotle's writings existed in translation in Latin Europe. It was largely through the Latin translations of Averroës' work that Aristotle's legacy was recovered in the Latin West. Averroës wrote commentaries on almost all of Aristotle's books except for the Politics, to which he did not have access. Hebrew translations of his texts had a lasting impact on Jewish philosophers, including Moses Maimonides.

Leading Scholastics like Thomas Aquinas, who had studied under German theologian and philosopher Albertus Magnus, thought of Averroës as so important that, instead of referring to him by name, they called him "The Commentator"; and Aristotle, "The Philosopher." These sobriquets became part of academia's parlance.

Another luminary of al-Ándalus was Ibn al-'Arabi (1165–1240), perhaps the most important Sufi mystic and philosopher, and widely regarded as a saint. He studied the Kabbalah and Christian thought and had a profound, albeit controversial, impact on Muslim mysticism, Sufi poetry, and even medieval Christian mysticism. Some 800 works bear his name, although only 110 (perhaps more) manuscripts survive. His masterpieces are the *Fuṣūṣ al-hikam* (*The Bezels of Wisdom*) and *Al-Futūḥāt al-Makkiyyah* (*The Meccan Revelations*). He lived in Seville for thirty years and eventually left Spain and traveled around the Mediterranean and Middle East, spending the last two decades of his life in Damascus (four years of which overlapped when Rumi was also there).

It was in al-Ándalus that Jewish, Islamic, and Christian philosophy and theology dialoged together, and their mystical traditions brushed up against each other. The interaction was rich, the likes of which were rarely seen; and humanity benefitted immensely from this discourse during an era of peaceful co-existence. Toledo, in fact, was known as the "City of the Three Cultures."

This *convivencia* ("co-existence") was not without its failures and spasms of brutal oppression; but, overall, it was remarkable for its time in history.[4]

The era of expansive Muslim rule eventually ended with the Battle of Las Navas de Tolosa in 1212, when Christian Spanish King Alfonso VIII was victorious over the Muslim Almohads, who had taken over rule of al-Ándalus. Córdoba was captured from the Moors in 1236; and Seville, in 1248, leaving only Granada in their hands. At the same time, the Portuguese *reconquista* drove the Moors from the southern Algarve region.[5]

Despite the succeeding territorial restrictions his predecessors imposed on Muslim rule, King Alfonso X (1221–1284) contributed to a renaissance in the Iberian Peninsula. Called Alfonso the Wise, he was an intellectual and a promoter of the sciences.

Throughout his reign, Alfonso employed Jewish, Christian, and Muslim scholars at his court in Toledo, primarily for translating books from Arabic and Hebrew into Latin and Castilian, an enterprise he personally oversaw. These scholars formed the *Escuela de Traductores de Toledo* (Toledo School of Translators). Their efforts promoted Castilian as a "learning language" in science and literature, and laid the foundation for the Spanish language.

Scholasticism

Scholasticism originally began as a technique to reconcile the philosophy of the ancient classical philosophers with medieval Christian theology. It was not a philosophy or theology *per se*, but a dialectical learning method, a reasoning tool to find the answer to a question or resolve a contradiction. Although its application was in medieval theology, Scholasticism was eventually applied to classical philosophy and other fields of study.

The mendicant orders, especially the Dominicans and Franciscans, despite being enlisted to counter heretical groups, and irrespective of their focus on poverty, preaching, and pastoral ministry, quickly produced high-powered Scholastic theologians, such as Alexander of Hales (Franciscan), Thomas Aquinas (Dominican), and Bonaventure (Franciscan). Aquinas began his *Summa Theologiae* in 1265, the basis of systematic Christian theological teaching at the time, but halted it eight years later, never completing it.

In addition, that epoch saw renewed study of Natural Philosophy. Scholars like Robert Grosseteste, considered the founder of the modern English intellectual tradition, and Roger Bacon, both of Oxford, sought to blend the scientific methods of Aristotle and Arabic scholars.

Jewish

After the fall of Jerusalem in the first century, Babylonia (contemporary-day Baghdad) became the focus for Judaism for more than a thousand years.

Eventually, Jewish intellectual life and religious scholarship declined there due to the external pressures of wars of conquest and lessening acceptance. Al-Ándalus, having developed its own brand of tolerance, stepped in as the new center of Jewish intellectual endeavors. Jewish poets and commentators contributed to its cultural life; the region was crucial to development of Jewish philosophy.

A stream of Jewish philosophers, cross-fertilizing with Muslim philosophers, culminated with the widely celebrated Jewish thinker of the Middle Ages, Moses Maimonides (1135–1205), though he did not actually do any of his writing in al-Ándalus because, when he was 13, his family fled persecution by the Almohads, who had taken over the region.

Other Places on the Globe

Persian

By the 13th century, a vibrant Persian culture extended across western, central, and southern Asia, even though inhabitants in this vast expanse had conflicting allegiances and spoke many different languages. Poets, artists, architects, artisans, jurists, and scholars, who maintained relations among their peers in the far-flung cities, spread the culture from Anatolia to India.

The invading Mongol armies challenged Persian culture during the 13th–15th centuries, ironically, stimulating cultural development in central and west Asia because of new geographic concentrations of artists and leaders created by those fleeing the invasions. Many Iranians, for example, sought refuge in a few safe havens, primarily India, where scholars, poets, musicians, and artisans mixed together.

After the imperial systems secured peace and travel was once again safe, scholars and artists, ideas and skills, and fine books and artifacts circulated freely over the extensive area. New styles of architecture based on pre-Islamic Iranian tradition developed. Persian literature was encouraged; and the Persian school of miniature painting (influenced by the Chinese) flourished, as did book production.

Abū-Muhammad Muslih al-Dīn bin Abdallāh Shīrāzī (Saadi Shirazi, or simply Saadi) became recognized as one of the greatest poets of the classical Persian literary tradition in the 13th century. Although known for the depth of his social and moral thought as a Sufi, he also excelled in Islamic theology, mysticism, sciences, law, governance, history, and Arabic literature.

Middle Eastern and Asian

Yunus Emre, Turkish poet and Sufi mystic (mid-1200s to early 1300s), exercised immense influence on Turkish literature. He was one of the first known poets to have composed in the spoken Turkish rather than in Persian or

Arabic. About the same time lived Ibn Taymiyyah, a famous Salafi Islamic scholar, philosopher, theologian, logician, and student of Sufism in eastern Turkey and Syria.

Other developments from this vast region include the use of ceramic Guan ware in China, during the Southern Song dynasty; and Xia Gui painted his famous Twelve Views from a Thatched Hut.

The late 13th century and early 14th centuries also gave light to the Japanese masterpieces, Night Attack on the Sanjo Palace, and Descent of the Amida Trinity, respectively, and the continuing evolution of Noh drama in Japan.

POLITICAL EVENTS

In 1215, a group of English nobles forced King John to sign the Magna Carta, which granted the British aristocracy the right of jury trial and protection from arbitrary acts by the King and began the English constitutional tradition. The nobility further limited the monarchy's power forty years later with the Provisions of Oxford. In 1282, Danish nobles compelled their own "Magna Carta," subordinating the king to parliament.

In other political developments during the last third of the 13th century, France saw a huge expansion of royal power (along with material and cultural advances); the Hapsburg dynasty was established and would last until 1918; Genoa was enjoying a golden age, the Swiss Confederation was founded (leading to the formation of Switzerland in 1353); Sweden conquered Finland and forced the Finns to convert to Christianity; the governing Great Council of the Venetian Republic was established; and the English, using long bows, successfully quelled a Scottish rebellion for independence lead by William Wallace.

Tamar the Great (Queen Regnant of Georgia from the 12th to 13th centuries) presided over the Georgian Golden Age of political and military successes and cultural achievements.

The Kingdom of Kediri, the dominant power in east Java, fell to the Singhasari regime in 1222, which then ruled seventy years, until the beginning of the Hindu Majapahit Empire that became a vast archipelagic Indonesian empire. The Sultanate of Ternate, one of the oldest Muslim kingdoms in Indonesia, came to power in 1257 and eventually encompassed most of eastern Indonesia and part of southern Philippines.

In 1238, the Sukhothai kingdom was founded in north central Thailand, and lasted a hundred years. The Mali Empire reached its height in Africa in the first half of the 14th century.

About the same time, the Aztecs (the Mexica, as they called themselves) had established Tenochtitlán, the site of contemporary Mexico City; and the

Toltecs were in decline. The Mayan confederacy was in place on the Yucatan peninsula and into Guatemala, and the Incas were settling into the Peruvian Andes. On Easter Island, the *moai* (giant stone heads) were still being fashioned, a project that lasted hundreds of years.

Elsewhere, the Adena and Hopewell peoples had organized themselves in the Middle Mississippi Valley (one of the centers, Cahokia, had 30,000 people). By that time, further to the west, the Pueblo people had finished abandoning their cliff dwellings.

13TH-CENTURY INVENTIONS

Various Chinese dynasties in power began use of land mines, rockets, explosive bombs, and hand cannons for warfare. By the end of the century, the Chinese had developed the first prototype canon. While the Chinese were at the forefront of the early use of gunpowder, it was the Europeans who soon developed pistols and other guns that gave them a decisive military advantage; and the use of gunpowder spread rapidly around the world.

The Chinese adopted the windmill from the Islamic world, and dominoes were first played in China. Eyeglasses were invented in Italy in 1286. The Chinese governmental minister Wang Zhen invented wooden movable type printing in 1298.

As a coda to this section, although not a new invention, the use of bank checks increased dramatically, particularly in Barcelona, Genoa, Florence, and Venice, to facilitate payment among merchants. Checking systems were already in use in the Muslim world by the 10th century. During the Crusades, Europeans increased their contacts with the banking and monetary systems of the Muslim eastern Mediterranean world and began to adopt and adapt them.

CONCLUDING COMMENTS

This era could be summed up much as Charles Dickens wrote in 1859 in *A Tale of Two Cities*: "It was the best of times, it was the worst of times, it was the age of wisdom, it was the age of foolishness, it was the epoch of belief, it was the epoch of incredulity, it was the season of Light, it was the season of Darkness, it was the spring of hope, it was the winter of despair . . . ."[6]

In this era of enormous, stunning intellectual progress and simultaneous fearsome calamities, the reprehensible paths taken by mainstream leadership is not surprising, nor was their propensity to cling to rigid theologies and politics of "us and them." Such tendencies occur in times of high anxiety, including in our own post-9/11 world.

On the other hand, for those unwilling to succumb to fundamentalist antidotes, the 13th and 14th centuries produced an insatiable interest in mysticism. This era, writes Professor Soltes, created "the search for passage out and elsewhere into the deepest Other."[7] Three mystics who took on the challenge to explore that deepest Other were Mevlana Rumi, Meister Eckhart, and Moses de León.

NOTES

1. There were other brutal and bloody crusades within Europe during the 13th century, sometimes with papal sanction, sometimes without, for a variety of religious, economic, and political motives, one example being the Albigensian Crusade in southern France against the Cathars.

2. For two exceptional articles on the Mongols, see "The Mongols in World History," Asian Topics in World History, Columbia University, http://afe.easia.columbia.edu/mongols/ and "The Mongols' Mark on Global History," Asian Topics in World History, Columbia University, http://afe.easia.columbia.edu/mongols/history/history.htm.

3. See Noah Gordon, *The Last Jew* (New York: St. Martin's Griffin, 2002), for an excellent novel about the expulsion of Jews from Spain.

4. For an overview of this *convivencia*, with its successes and failures, tolerance and oppression, see Chris Lowney, *A Vanished World: Muslims, Christians, and Jews in Medieval Spain* (Oxford, UK: Oxford University Press, 2006).

5. Toledo had fallen to Alfonso VI of Castile in 1085, as the first major city in the Christian Reconquista.

6. Charles Dickens, *A Tale of Two Cities* (Mineola, NY: Dover Publications, 1998), 1.

7. Ori Z. Soltes, *Mysticism in Judaism, Christianity, and Islam: Searching for Oneness* (Lanham, MD: Rowman & Littlefield, 2009), 143.

Chapter Five

Jalal ad-Din Rumi

People pray to You from fear of the Fire;
And, if You do not cast them into the Fire,
that is their reward.
Or they pray for the Garden,
full of fruits and flowers;
and that is their prize.
But I do not pray to You like this,
for I am not afraid of the Fire;
nor do I ask for the Garden.
All I want is your Love,
and to return to be One with You,
and become your Face.

—Rabi`a al-Adawiya

Jalāl ad-Dīn Muhammad Balkhī (also, Jalāl ad-Dīn Muhammad Rūmī) (1207–1273), popularly known simply as Rumi in the English-speaking world, was a poet, jurist, philosopher, theologian, and, most importantly, a Sufi mystic. His life was as passionate as his poetry[1]; and he is widely revered as a Sufi saint.

Rumi is commonly referred to with the respectful title Mevlâna in modern Turkey (and is what will be used in the following dialogs). It roughly translates as "our master" or "our teacher." In Muslim countries, he is more generally identified by his full name or as *Mawlavi* (Persian), which means "having to do with the master."[2] His teachings provide one of the best introductions to Sufi philosophy and practice, and the pithy brilliance of his mystical poetry is unmatched in eloquence and poignancy.

Jalal ad-Din Rumi lived most of his life in Konya in the Anatolia region of contemporary Turkey, which had been part of the Byzantine or eastern Roman Empire and which Muslims only recently had conquered. The area was known to Arabs, Persians, and Turks as Rûm, a term borrowed from Arabic, literally meaning "Roman."

Rumi was born to native Persian-speaking parents in an area that is now Tajikistan, which belonged to Balkh province (part of which is in contemporary Afghanistan), a center of a Persian culture with its own brand of Sufism that had developed over several centuries.

Rumi's father was Bahāud-Dīn Walad, a highly respected theologian, jurist, and mystic, to whom Rumi's followers reverently referred to as Sultan al-Ulama ("Sultan of the Scholars"). He came from several generations of Islamic preachers of the liberal Hanafi rite, a family tradition that Rumi carried on. His father's mystical writings describe a remarkably sensual union with God.

When the Mongols invaded Central Asia in the early 12th century, Bahaud-Din Walad, along with family and disciples, set out westward. According to a hagiographical narrative, Rumi met the renowned Persian mystic poet Attar in the Iranian city of Nishapur, who immediately recognized Rumi's spiritual eminence. Attar saw Bahaud-Din walking ahead of his son and said, "Here comes a sea, followed by an ocean." He gave the boy his *Asrārnāma*, a book about entanglement of the soul with the material world. According to this popular account, the meeting had a deep impact on the 18-year-old Rumi and was an inspiration for him.

From Nishapur, the Bahaud-Din entourage went to Baghdad, meeting scholars and Sufis there, and then migrated to various other cities. In 1225, Rumi married and had two sons, Sultan Walad and 'Ala' ud-Din Chalabi, who would later figure prominently in his life. Rumi's wife died at an unknown date, and he married again and had another son and a daughter.

In May 1228, Bahaud-Din and his group settled in Konya, within the westernmost Seljuk Sultanate of Rûm. There, Bahaud-Din became the head of a *madrassa* (religious school). He died in 1231; and Rumi, age 25, inherited his position and trained in the Shari'a (Islamic religious law and moral code) and the *tariqa* (mystical "path"),[3] as his father had taught those disciplines.

During this period, Rumi traveled to Aleppo and then Damascus, where he remained four years. His time in Damascus overlapped with the last years of Ibn al-'Arabi's life. The latter, one of the era's preeminent Sufi masters, had migrated there from al-Ándalus (Moorish Spain). Rumi returned to Konya in 1240, where, as an accomplished Islamic jurist and a *molvi* (Islamic teacher), he began preaching in Konya's mosques and the madrassa.

Rumi met the dervish Shams of Tabriz in November 1244, an event that radically altered Rumi's life. Shams (1185–1248) was a Persian Muslim mystic and had traveled throughout the Middle East searching and praying for a teacher who could, as he put it, "endure my company."[4] Rumi's transformation from an established Islamic scholar into a Sufi mystic grew out of this encounter and his ongoing spiritual relationship with Shams, who was thirty years his senior. It was said theirs was "a meeting of two great rivers."

During the evening of December 5, 1248, according to one tradition, while Rumi and Shams were talking at Rumi's residence, Shams was called to the back door. He went out, and was never seen again. One rumor was that Rumi's disciples, jealous of his relationship with Shams, murdered him, perhaps with assistance from Rumi's son 'Ala' ud-Din. Another account is that, after several years with Rumi in Konya, Shams simply left suddenly and settled in Khoy (present-day Iran), where he died. There is a tomb for him in Khoy, as well as in Konya.

As the years passed, Rumi attributed more and more of his own poetry to Shams as a sign of love for his departed friend and master. In Rumi's poetry, Shams becomes a guide of Allah's love for humankind; Shams was a sun ("Shams" means "Sun" in Arabic), shining the Light of Sun as a beacon of the right path for Rumi.[5] In some respects, Shams functioned as a stand-in for God in Rumi's poetry.

Rumi expressed his love and bereavement for Shams in a torrent of lyric poems, *Divan-e Shams-e Tabrizi*. He even went to Damascus searching for Shams, where he finally came to terms with his loss through a kind of self-realization:

> Why am I seeking? I am the same as He.
> His essence speaks through me.
> I have been looking for myself![6]

Rumi eventually found another companion in Salaḥud-Din-e Zarkub, a goldsmith. After Salaḥud's death, Rumi's scribe and favorite student, Hussam-e Chalabi, assumed the companion role.

One day, the story goes, as the two were wandering through a vineyard outside Konya, Hussam suggested that Rumi write a book of mystical poetry that "would become the companion of many troubadours. They would fill their hearts from your work and compose music to accompany it." Rumi smiled and took out a piece of paper on which he already had written the opening eighteen lines of his *Masnavi*, a lyrical masterwork, beginning with: "Listen to the reed and the tale it tells, How it sings of separation . . . ."[7] Rumi spent the next twelve years dictating the six volumes of the *Masnavi*, to him.

In December 1273, Jalal ad-Din Rumi fell ill; he predicted his own death and composed the well-known *ghazal* (a Persian form of verse, usually dealing with love), which begins with:

> How do you know what sort of king
> I have within me as companion?
> Do not cast your glance upon my golden face,
> for I have iron legs.[8]

Rumi died on December 17 and was laid to rest alongside his father. Christians and Jews joined his funeral procession. A well-appointed shrine, the *Yeşil Türbe* ("Green Tomb"), was erected over his place of burial with the epitaph: "When we are dead, seek not our tomb in the earth, but find it in the hearts of men." The shrine, with its mosque, dance hall, dervish living quarters, school, and tombs of some leaders of the Mevlevi Order, draws pilgrims from around the world.[9]

TEACHINGS

Konya, where Jalal ad-Din Rumi lived and taught most of his life, was a diverse community; Christians, Jews, and Muslims, as well as Romans, Turks, and Arabs, all lived together fairly harmoniously. This helped shape Rumi's universalism. Rumi saw common values in Islamic, Jewish, and Christian teachings, such as love, peace, sisterhood/brotherhood, forgiveness, mercy, and spiritual purification.

These common universal values, for Rumi, reflected that the love of God brought peace within human societies, nature, and one's spiritual life. Rumi's teachings of unbounded tolerance, progressive reasoning, goodness, charity, and awareness through love have appealed to people of all sects and creeds, and even to those with no particular belief system.

The essence of Rumi's thought generally emanates from the Sufi concept of *tawhid*[10] —union with the Beloved, from whom one has come and been cut off, and now in loneliness, longs to restore union. The spirit of this concept is felt in the longing of the reed to return to the reed bed in the *Masnavi*, one of his preeminent compositions:

> Ever since they cut me from the reed bed,
> my wail has caused men and women to weep . . . .
> . . . .
> Whoever has been parted from his source
> longs to return to that state of Union.[11]

Rumi believed the spirit, after devolution from the divine Ego, undergoes an evolutionary process by which it comes nearer and nearer to the same divine Ego. All matter in the universe obeys this law, and this movement is due to an inbuilt urge (which Rumi calls "love") in people to evolve and seek union with the Divine from which they have emerged. He reinterpreted the account of the Fall of Adam as the devolution of the Ego from the universal ground of Divinity, itself a universal, cosmic phenomenon.[12] Rumi believed that, in the process of achieving union with God, God is both the ground and goal of all existence.

Rumi was concerned with human beings' spiritual evolution. A person who is not conscious of God is akin to an animal; true consciousness makes the person divine. Some have seen this as a Neoplatonic doctrine: the universal soul working through the various spheres of being, a teaching introduced into Islam by Muslim philosophers like al-Farabi (known in the West as Alpharabius) and related to the concept of love of Ibn Sina (familiar in the West as Avicenna), a magnetic-like power that pulls life upward toward the Beloved.

The Sufi tradition to which Jalal ad-Din Rumi belonged and helped create (and there are many different Sufi traditions in Islam) saw life as a path to the Divine on which we use all our abilities to get closer to God, which would be perfection. It is a journey into oneself, one's heart, and one's soul. The journey involves acquiring moral attributes, practicing austerity and sincerity, and resisting carnal temptations.

This personal reorientation focuses the heart in a "compass-like" direction toward God. As Rumi expresses it in the *Masnavi*: "The lover's cause is separate from all other causes. Love is the astrolabe of God's mysteries."[13]

The crucial goal of searching for the Divine is being together with God and living in God's presence, and not entertaining any worldly goal or distractions. This means seeing behind the "outer" appearances of things and events and interpreting whatever happens in the world in relation to God. Every part of life, then, is to be present with God and thus worship God, which we do with tongue, heart, and soul, regardless of the externalities of formal religion.

One of Rumi's famous poems powerfully expresses that the Beloved is within us, not exterior to us, regardless of philosophical or religious practice:

> I tried to find Him on the Christian cross, but He was not there;
> I went to the temple of the Hindus and to the old pagodas,
> but I could not find a trace of Him anywhere . . . .
> I searched on the mountains and in the valleys,
> but neither in the heights nor in the depths was I able to find Him.
> I went to the Ka'bah in Mecca, but He was not there either . . . .
> I questioned the scholars and philosophers,
> But He was beyond their understanding . . . .
> Then I looked into my heart, and it was there
> where He dwelled that I saw Him.
> He was nowhere else to be found.[14]

Jalal ad-Din Rumi's teachings are ecumenical in nature. For him, religion was essentially a personal, spiritual experience beyond logical argument and sense perception. Creative love, or the impulse to rejoin the spirit to Divinity, was the goal toward which everything moves. The dignity of life, in particular human life (which is conscious of its divine origin and goal), was therefore important: "The nation of Love has a different religion of all religions. For lovers, God alone is their religion."

Although Rumi was a universalist, his own spiritual practice was Islamic, albeit unique, based on the Qur'an, the *hadith* (teachings of the Prophet Muhammad relayed by tradition), and the *sunna* (life of Muhammad). His brand of Sufism, while reflecting almost five centuries of Sufi thought, diverged from traditional Sufis with his emphasis on personal independent reasoning and focus on the love of God.

Despite his ecumenical attitude, Rumi was not a proponent of non-denominational spirituality. He believed in the importance of religious observance and the Qur'an's primacy:

> Flee to God's Qur'an, take refuge in it;
> there with the spirits of the prophets merge.
> The Book conveys the prophets' circumstances;
> those fish of the pure sea of Majesty. [15]

MAJOR WORKS

Rumi has two poetic masterpieces, both already mentioned. One is the *Maṭnawīye Ma'nawī* (or *Mesnevi, Masnavi, Spiritual Couplets*), a six-volume poem (almost 26,000 couplets), regarded by some Sufis as the Persian-language Qur'an[16]; many consider this to be one of the grandest creations of mystical poetry in Persian, a literary glory. The *Masnavi* weaves fables, anecdotes, tales, Qur'anic revelations, *hadith* exegesis, and spiritual insights into an elegantly intricate tapestry.

Rumi's other premier opus is the *Dīvān-e Kabīr* (*Great Work*) or *Dīvān-e Shams-e Tabrīzī* (*The Works of Shams of Tabriz*), named in honor of his spiritual companion. The *Divan* encompasses approximately 35,000 couplets, 2,000 quatrains in Persian, 90 *ghazals*, 19 quatrains in Arabic, a few dozen or so couplets in Turkish (mainly macaronic poems in mixed Persian and Turkish), and 14 couplets in Greek (in three macaronic poems in Greek and Persian). [17]

A third work is *Fihi ma Fihi* (*It Is What It Is*), a collection of seventy-one prose, colloquial works, divided into *The Discourses, The Letters,* and *The Seven Sermons,* directed toward students and followers and compiled from their notes. They are Rumi's own writings.

The Sermons (*Majāles-e Sab'a*), written in simple, but elegant, Persian, are seven reflections on the meaning of the Qur'an and *hadith.* Rumi's use of Arabic and knowledge of history show his facility in Islamic sciences. His style is typical of the genre of Sufis and spiritual teachers.

The Letters (*Makatib*), epistolary in style, are in Persian and addressed to his disciples, family members, and persons of governance and influence.

They also show Rumi helping family members and administering the community of followers that had grown up around him.

ORDER OF WHIRLING DERVISHES

Following Jalal ad-Din Rumi's death, his followers and his son Sultan Walad, author of the mystical *Maṭnawī Rabābnāma* (*Book of the Rabab*), founded the Mevlevi Order, which became famous for its Sufi dance (the *Sama* ceremony, also known as the Whirling Dervishes). Hussam Chalabi was its first leader. After his death in 1284, Sultan Walad took over leadership, which has remained within Rumi's family in Konya ever since.

A dervish is a person who has purified the self of worldly desires; the Mevlevi Sufis forsake materialism in their journey to God and learn a life of love and service to people. They originally wore simple woolen clothing as a sign of austerity and simplicity. They are known for their famous invitation to people of all backgrounds:

> Come, come, whoever you are,
> wanderer, idolater, worshiper of fire.
> Come, even though you have broken
> your vows a thousand times.
> Come, and come yet again.
> Ours is not a caravan of despair.

Rumi passionately believed in using music, poetry and dance as a path to God.[18] For him, music helped individuals focus their being on the Divine, so intensely in fact, that the soul was both destroyed and resurrected. These beliefs led to the Sama's whirling dervishes evolving into ritual form as a sacred dance. The music accompanying the Sama consists of settings of poems from the *Masnavi* and *Dīvān-e Kabīr* or Sultan Walad's poems.

The dervishes perform the Sama to music, notably from a reed flute, known as a *ney*. The dervishes and audience form a three-part body in the Sama performance. The ney represents the human voice, lamenting separation in this material world from God, with whom we seek to be united now and hereafter. The symbolic use of the reed in the *Masnavi* was referenced earlier. The "Samazens" spin counterclockwise, with one hand reaching toward the heavens and the other hand toward the earth. The gesture symbolizes the link between the material and spiritual worlds. The hand toward heaven transmits God's love to earth with the other hand.[19]

The Sama represents a mystical path of spiritual ascent through love to the Perfect One.[20] In this journey, the seeker symbolically turns toward the truth, grows through love, abandons the ego, finds the truth, and arrives at the Perfect. The seeker then returns from this spiritual experience with greater maturity, to love and to be of service to the whole of creation without discrimination, regardless of the belief, nationality, race, or class of others in the community.

Mustafa Kemal Atatürk, after founding the modern, secular Republic of Turkey in 1923, excluded religion from the public sphere, restricting it to personal morals and faith. A 1925 law closed dervish lodges and pilgrimage centers of veneration.[21] The law dissolved the Sufi orders, prohibited use of mystical names, titles, and costumes, impounded the orders' assets, and banned their ceremonies and meetings. Two years later, however, the Rumi mausoleum was permitted to reopen as a museum.

In the 1950s, the Turkish government allowed the Whirling Dervishes to perform once a year in Konya. The Mevlana festival is held in early December and culminates on December 17, the Urs of Mevlana (anniversary of Rumi's death), called *Šabe Arūs* (Persian for "nuptial night"), the night of Rumi's union with God.

In 1974, the Whirling Dervishes were authorized to travel to the West for the first time. In 2005, UNESCO proclaimed the "The Mevlevi Sama Ceremony" of Turkey as one of the Masterpieces of the Oral and Intangible Heritage of Humanity.[22]

LEGACY

Although much still remains to be translated, Rumi's work has found its way into many of the world's languages and in any number of formats, such as concerts, readings, dance performances, and other artistic renditions.[23] Coleman Barks' acclaimed performance interpretations of Rumi's poetry have sold more than half a million copies worldwide, and Rumi is one of the most widely read poets in Canada and the United States.

The cultural, historical, and linguistic ties between Rumi and Iran also have made him an iconic Iranian poet. Some preeminent Rumi scholars have come from present-day Iran, where his poetry is displayed on the walls of many cities, sung in Persian music, and read in schools. Rumi's poetry also resonates in classical Iranian and Afghan music, especially the Eastern-Persian and Tajik-Hazara variety.

Jalal ad-Din Rumi sears as deeply into the hearts of the 21st century, as he so passionately touched the souls of those before us.

NOTES

1. For a superb and elegant summary of Rumi's life and thought, see Ori Z. Soltes, *Embracing the World: Fethullah Gülen's Thought and Its Relationship to Jalaluddin Rumi and Others* (Clifton, NJ: Tughra Books, 2013), Chap. 2, 19–49.

2. When dealing with Rumi and his era, all sorts of variants of English spelling present themselves. This occurs in part because of the various languages involved (older and newer versions of Turkish, Persian, and Arabic) and the effort to transliterate accurately the pronunciation sounds into current-day English. This happens frequently, for example, with the choices of the English "v" or "w."

3. *Tariqa* ("path," or "way") is the Muslim spiritual path toward direct knowledge of God. Originally, *tariqa* meant the spiritual path of individual Sufi mystics. By the 13th century, as Sufi communities gathered around teachers, *tariqa* came to designate the entire ritual system followed by the community or mystic order. Eventually, *tariqa* came to mean the order itself.

4. Shams is author of the *Maqalat-e Shams-e Tabrizi* (*Discourse of Shams-i Tabrīzī*), a Persian prose book with a mystical interpretation of Islam and spiritual advice.

5. See satash8, "Rumi's Sun: Shams Tabrizi," June 14, 2013, https://www.youtube.com/watch?v=kY5qU0Dfpao.

6. Rumi, *The Essential Rumi*, trans. Coleman Barks and John Moyne (New York: HarperOne, 2004), xx.

7. Rumi, "Listen to the Reed," *I Love Rumi*, Dec. 28, 2010, http://www.experience project.com/stories/Love-Rumi/1331136.

8. Seyyed Hossein Nasr, *Islamic Art and Spirituality* (New York: SUNY Press, 1987), 120.

9. Travel in Turkey, "Mevlana Museum," March 9, 2013, https://www.youtube.com/watch?v=Jtr1A69PBr0. Rumi and his mausoleum were depicted on the 1981–1994 Turkish 5000 lira banknotes.

10. *Tawhid*, in Islam, means the oneness of God and also refers to the nature of that God as a unity, apart from creation. For Muslim mystics and Sufis, however, *tawhid* has a panentheistic sense, that God is present in all of creation. Generally, Muslim scholars view the science of *tawhid* as a systematic theology toward a better knowledge of God; but Sufis believe that God can be reached only through spiritual experience.

11. See "Translations and Versions of 'The Song of the Reed' (*Masnavi*, Book 1: Lines 1–34)," *Dar-Al-Masnavi of the Mevlevi Order*, http://www.dar-al-masnavi.org/reedsong.html.

12. M.M. Sharif, *A History of Muslim Philosophy*, Internet Archive, Community Books, https://archive.org/details/HistoryOfMuslimPhilosophy (vol. 2, 827, 828).

13. Majid M. Naini, *Mysteries of the Universe and Rumi's Discoveries on the Majestic Path of Love*, Universal Vision Research, 2002, http://www.naini.net/main.htm.

14. This quotation is widely ascribed to Rumi, and not disputed. Professor Soltes notes that many Rumi poems are validated, among other reasons, by being unequivocally attributed him, conveying the same thoughts. Ori Z. Soltes, *Embracing the World: Fethullah Gülen's Thought and Its Relationship to Jalaluddin Rumi and Others* (Clifton, NJ: Tughra Books, 2013), 34 n. 58. For a daily poem or photograph, see Rumi's Facebook Page, "Timeline Photos," https://www.facebook.com/mevlana/photos/a.424140758184.199763.64655903184/10152737893258185/?type=1.

15. Franklin Lewis, *Rumi: Past and Present, East and West—The Life, Teachings, and Poetry of Jalal al-Din Rumi* (London: Oneworld Publications, 2000), 408.

16. One of the greatest authorities on Rumi, Hâdî Hâ'irî, has shown in an unpublished work that some 6,000 verses of the *Divan* and the *Masnavi* are practically direct translations of Qur'anic verses into Persian poetry. The 15th-century Sufi poet Jâmî, said the *Masnavi* is the Qur'an in the Persian tongue.

17. For an eloquent rendition of four of Rumi's poems that help summarize his mystic insight, see Andrew Harvey, "Andrew Harvey on Rumi," http://player.vimeo.com/video/90455187. YouTube has many wonderful artistic renditions of Rumi's poetry.

18. According to tradition, Rumi himself played the *robāb* (similar to a lute), although his favorite instrument was the *ney* or reed flute.

19. See Smithsonian, "A Spiritual Offering: Whirling Dervishes of the Istanbul Historical Turkish Music Community," http://www.youtube.com/watch?v=JiqCnNv5zbk (a 40-minute spiritual dance, with an introduction and reading from Rumi).

20. Dia Sehgal, "Rumi's love poems," https://www.youtube.com/playlist?list=PL8503774127FC5EE4.

21. Istanbul alone had more than 250 Sufi lodges, as well as smaller gathering centers for various Sufi-related fraternities.

22. "The Mevlevi Sema Ceremony," *UNESCO*, 2005, http://www.unesco.org/culture/intangible-heritage/39eur_uk.htm.

23. See "Unself Yourself," "Shams of Tabriz—The Forty Rules of Love," July 6, 2013, https://www.youtube.com/watch?v=saPd2WDJ4xI, based on the novel, Elif Shafak, *Forty Rules of Love: A Novel of Rumi* (New York: Viking Books, 2010).

Chapter Six

Meister Eckhart

I pray God rid me of God.

Meister Eckhart (Eckhart von Hochheim) (ca. 1260–ca. 1327) is one of the best known Christian mystics; he was also a philosopher, theologian, and priest of the Dominican Order. Since the mid-19th century, his works have regained the popularity they had when he was alive and for a while afterwards.

Eckhart was a well-respected preacher, dealing with themes such as the nature of God, the Trinity, the relationship of the human soul to God, sin and redemption, Christ, and ethics.[1] His views crept away from orthodoxy at times, which caused problems with ecclesiastical authorities. He inspired both admiration and suspicion, depending on the audience.

Much about Eckhart's early life is unclear. He was born near Gotha in the Landgraviate of Thuringia in the Holy Roman Empire. He joined the Dominicans at Erfurt, probably around age 18. He likely studied at Cologne and at the University of Paris, and came to hold positions in Dominican leadership.

Eckhart begins to emerge in 1294 while a theology lecturer on the *Sentences* of Peter Lombard, who greatly influenced Scholastic theologians of the Middle Ages. In 1300, he went to teach in Paris, eventually holding the Dominican Chair of Theology, and returned to Erfurt in late 1303. Thereafter, he held various leadership positions in the Dominican Order for its provinces in Saxony and Bohemia to reform the demoralized monasteries there. He established three convents for women during his tenure.

In 1311, Eckhart was invited back to the University of Paris as a *magister* (teacher), a rare honor previously held only by Thomas Aquinas. He lived in Paris for two academic years until summer 1313, staying in the same house as fellow Dominican William of Paris, the Inquisitor of France, who had ordered Marguerite Porete, a French mystic and spirituality author, burned at the stake in 1310 for heresy.

Then much of what is known about Eckhart's life is blank again, only that he was in Strasbourg some of the time, essentially concerned with spiritual direction and preaching for Dominican communities. He may have taught in Frankfurt, as well. In late 1323 or early 1324, Eckhart left Strasbourg for the Dominican house at Cologne, where he may have lectured some at the city's prestigious Studium.

Eckhart continued to preach during a period of disarray among the clergy and monastic orders, rapid growth of numerous pious lay groups, and the Inquisition's continuing anxieties over "heretical" movements throughout Europe, which were part of the pre-Reformation stew that was beginning to simmer.

Church authorities worried about Eckhart's teaching. The Dominican General Chapter in Venice in 1325 had spoken out against "friars in Teutonia [Germanic region] who say things in their sermons that can easily lead simple and uneducated people into error."[2] Eckhart was clearly the target since he deliberately preached in the vernacular so that everyone, not just those schooled in Latin, could understand his sermons.

This alarmed fellow Dominican Nicholas of Strasbourg, himself a mystic, to whom the pope had entrusted the temporary charge of German Dominican monasteries. To protect Eckhart, he conducted an investigation of his orthodoxy and presented a list of suspect passages from Eckhart's *Book of Consolation* to him.[3] Eckhart responded with a (now lost) treatise *Requisitus*, which satisfied his immediate superiors of his orthodoxy.

Despite this assurance, the Archbishop of Cologne, Henry of Virneburg, ordered an inquisitorial process in 1326, led by the Franciscan Order, which was in increasing tension with Eckhart's Dominican friars. At this point, Eckhart issued a *Vindicatory Document*, providing chapter and verse of what he taught.

Throughout the difficult months of late 1326, Eckhart had the full support of local Dominican authorities, as evident in Nicholas' three official protests in January 1327 against the inquisitors' actions.

In February 1327, before the archbishop's local inquisitors pronounced sentence, Eckhart preached a sermon in the Dominican church at Cologne, and then had his secretary read aloud a public protestation of his innocence. It generally stated he had always detested everything erroneous; and, should anything of the kind be found in his writings, he retracted it. Eckhart himself translated the text into German so all the congregation could understand it, probably to protect himself from any accusation that he said one thing in Latin, and another in German.

The verdict went against Eckhart. He then denied the competence and authority of the inquisitors and the archbishop, and set off on a 600-mile trip to Avignon, the location of the papacy at the time, in a bid to appeal directly to the pope.

What happened at Avignon with Pope John XXII is not completely clear because documentation is scant; but, at some point, the 150 suspect articles or charges against Eckhart were whittled down to 28. The papal commission eventually confirmed, in modified form, the decision of the Cologne Inquisition against Eckhart; but he had died in the meantime before the judgment could issue against him.

In March 1329, more than a year after Eckhart's death, the pope issued a bull (*In Agro Dominico*), which characterized a series of Eckhart's statements as heretical or suspect, but did not condemn him personally as a heretic. This unusual *post mortem* process may have reflected the hierarchy's fear of what it viewed as the growing problem of the "heresy" of mysticism.

INFLUENCE

Eckhart remained widely read in the later Middle Ages. However, his trial (he was the only medieval theologian whom the Inquisition tried as a heretic) and subsequent papal condemnation of excerpts from his work cast a pall over his reputation.

The lay group Friends of God, which existed in communities across the region, carried on Eckhart's ideas under the leadership of local priests. Likewise, members of the Dominican and Carthusian religious orders continued to read Eckhart well after his death.

Nicholas of Cusa, who lived in the 15th century and became Archbishop of Cologne, and also a mystic, studied Eckhart extensively.[4] Nicholas wrote *De Pace Fidei* after the conquest of Constantinople in 1453, a startling dialog seeking peace among world religions, which had a discussion to the effect that God created all religions and all religions lead back to God.

Eckhart's practical communication of the mystical path is believed to be behind the influential 14th-century "anonymous" *Theologia Germanica,*[5] a mystical treatise that circulated after his death. The lack of church imprimatur and anonymity of the author did not lessen its influence for the next two centuries, including on Martin Luther at the peak of resistance to the papal indulgence scandal.

WORKS AND TEACHINGS

Thereafter, Eckhart's work generally receded from view until a revival in the early 19th century, especially by the German Romantics and Idealist philosophers. Both Franz Pfeiffer, who published Eckhart's German sermons and treatises in 1857, and Heinrich Seuse Denifle, who was the first to recover Eckhart's Latin works, ultimately helped propel modern-day interest in Eckhart.

Since his "rediscovery," Eckhart has acquired the status of a great mystic within popular spirituality. Scholars generally place him squarely in medieval Scholastic and philosophical traditions and agree that he falls within the tradition of philosophical mysticism of Plato, Plotinus, and Neoplatonist thinkers.

There are two ongoing questions about Eckhart's works: which are genuinely his, and whether his German or Latin works should have greater authoritative weight?

Questions as to the authenticity of the German sermons arise because many are versions written down by others from memory or notes. Of Eckhart's 86 extant sermons considered genuine, only 24 are indisputably authentic, as are only four of his vernacular treatises.

Unlike the vernacular works, which survive in more than 200 manuscripts, only a handful of manuscripts of his Latin treatises remain. However, they are critical to understanding Eckhart since he carefully crafted them for publication. The Latin works are considered authentic.

Eckhart's existing Latin writings represent only a small portion of what he had planned to write. He had intended to author a vast *Opus Tripartitum* (*Three-Part Work*). Unfortunately, all that exists today of the first part, the *Work of Propositions*, is the prologue. The second part, the *Work of Questions*, no longer exists. The third part, the *Work of Commentaries*, his major surviving Latin work, has a prologue, six commentaries, and fifty-six sermons.

In the early 20th century, Eckhart's *Defense* (also known as the *Rechtsfertigung, Vindicatory Document*) emerged. It records his responses to two of the series of charges against him at the Cologne trial. It supplied additional extra details of his trial, and provided authentication for some of his vernacular sermons and treatises.

Sermons

Although a distinguished theologian, Eckhart is best-remembered for his unusual sermons in German. As a preaching friar, he attempted to guide lay people, as well as monks and nuns under his care, with practical sermons on spiritual transformation and New Testament metaphor related to the creative power inherent in disinterest or detachment. The first of Eckhart's cycle of four sermons on the eternal birth of the Word in the ground of the soul sums up the most important aspects of his teaching on spiritual maturity.[6]

Eckhart drew extensively on mythic imagery, and his sermons were notable for communicating the allegorical content of the Gospels. Eckhart intended his sermons to inspire individuals to desire the goal of leading a good life. He frequently used unusual language, which caused ecclesiastical authorities to suspect he was straying from their narrow path of orthodoxy.

The central theme of the sermons is the presence of God in the individual soul, and the dignity of the soul of the just person.[7] Eckhart typically elaborated on this theme, but rarely departed from it. One sermon in particular summarizes his message well:

> When I preach, I usually speak of detachment and say that a [person] should be empty of self and all things; and secondly, that [the individual] should be reconstructed in the simple good that God is; and thirdly, that [the person] should consider the great aristocracy which God has set up in the soul, such that by means of it [the individual] may wonderfully attain to God; and fourthly, of the purity of the divine nature.[8]

For Eckhart, God is primarily bountiful or fertile. From abundance of love, God gives birth to the Son, the Word in all of us. This is similar to the Neoplatonic notion of "ebullience" or "boiling over" of the One that cannot hold back its copiousness of Being. But, in Eckhart's view, creation is not a "compulsory" overflowing; it is the free act of will by the triune nature of Deity.

Another provocative Eckhart insight is his distinction between God and Godhead (meaning "Godhood" or "Godness," the state of being God), a divergence between the Manifest and Unmanifest Absolute. These notions are present in Pseudo-Dionysius' writings[9] and John Scotus' *De Divisione Naturae*, but Eckhart boldly refashioned them. It is also a distinction that appears in the Kabbalah, described later in this book. Eckhart says the difference between Godhead and God is like the difference between heaven and earth.

Finding God Within

In Eckhart's view, whatever we may seem to be doing or however far we may seem to be from the mark, we are really searching for God. If we go out of ourselves to find or fetch God, we make a mistake because we cannot find God outside ourselves. We should not conceive of God except as in us.

The Birth of the Word

Eckhart's most distinctive teaching is probably that the eternal birth of the Word from the Father is "now born in time, in human nature," that, if nothing separates our souls and God, the birth of the hidden Word can take place in the depths of our souls. He refers to this over and again in his sermons. Eckhart writes, "From all eternity God lies on a maternity bed giving birth. The essence of God is birthing."[10]

However, we must change for this birth to take place in us. As Eckhart says at the beginning of that sermon: "We shall therefore speak of this birth, of how it may take place in us and be consummated in the virtuous soul, whenever God the Father speaks his eternal Word in the perfect soul."[11]

An indispensable condition for this birth of God is to live a good Christian life, in which life, justice, and equality are begotten and become manifest as the Son. Eckhart distrusts rigid programs or systems for progressing in the spiritual life, saying there is no single "way" to God, for God to be born in us—contrary to what spiritual luminaries down the centuries have taught.

What he does stress is that, before anything else, we must be utterly passive. But this is different from being weak, lethargic, or negative. The eternal birth takes place in the depths of the self, of the soul, beyond our senses; and it is with God's help that we acquire the capability to empty the mind inwardly of all sense experience, of all that pulls us out of ourselves.

Nor does the withdrawal and passivity required for the birth necessarily involve the "rapture" or "ecstasy" of which some mystics speak. In fact, there is also a "dark way" to God, one that is not readily revealed, that has absolute priority. John of the Cross calls this the "dark night of the soul."[12] It is the nature of the Divine Word to be hidden in its revelation and revealed in its hiddenness.

For Eckhart, reaching the state of passivity is no easy task. It is laborious and demands both physical seclusion and the ability to jettison the ideas whirling around in the head. One must still the body to still the mind.

If we can learn to let ourselves go, we are in effect letting everything go. Total letting go is the way to gain all things in God, who is the real being of all. "The person who would save his or her soul must lose it,"[13] is one of Eckhart's favorite Jesus sayings. He tells us:

> Now God wants no more from you than that you should in creaturely fashion go out of yourself, and let God be God in you . . . . Go completely out of yourself for God's love, and God comes completely out of [God's]self for love of you . . . . God must act and pour God's self into us when we are ready, in other words when we are totally empty of self and creatures. So stand still and do not waver from your emptiness.[14]

Eckhart rejected the centuries-old predominant notion about mysticism that we can only share God's life at a deep level by leading a reclusive existence, like in a monastery, that the active life was something to be endured and escaped from whenever possible. Eckhart passionately believed that the Divine Word can be born in an individual, even while absorbed in the harried world of daily existence:

Whoever truly possesses God in the right way possesses God in all places: on the street, in any company, as well as in a church or a remote place or in their cell . . . . Grasping all things in a divine way and making of them something more than they are in themselves cannot be learned by taking flight, but rather we must learn to maintain an inner solitude regardless of where we are or who we are with.

. . . .

Either a person must find God in works or abandon all works; but, since people cannot in this life be without works, they must learn to possess God in all things. [15]

Sermon 55 describes a life of detachment from the self and pure attachment to God alone:

You should never pray for any transitory thing; but, if you would pray for anything, you should pray for God's will alone and nothing else, and then you get everything. If you pray for anything else, you will get nothing. In God there is nothing but one, and one is indivisible. If you seek or expect anything more, that is not God but a fraction. You should seek nothing at all, neither knowledge nor understanding nor inwardness nor piety nor repose [yes, not even repose!] but only God's will. If you seek God's will alone, whatever flows from that or is revealed by that you may take as a gift from God without ever looking or considering whether it is by nature or grace or where it comes from or in what guise. And you need only lead an ordinary Christian life without considering doing anything special. [16]

Eckhart is famous for his controversial sermon about the Gospel story of Martha and Mary. His heroine is not the contemplative Mary, who only wanted to sit at Jesus' feet and be immersed in his presence, but the overworked Martha, whom Luke describes as "distracted by her many tasks." [17]

Eckhart argued that, in a life lived out in the world, a spirituality rooted in activity rather than vision can be a higher form of spirituality than traditional contemplative practice—at least, the contemplative ecstasy of Mary's kind, which is untethered to ordinary everyday life—something completely at odds with the traditional monastic-preferred teachings of Augustine, Gregory, Benedict, and Bernard.

This is the first time since Christianity's early days that a theologian articulated a spirituality of the active life, abandoning the long-prevailing conviction of an irreconcilable tension between contemplative and active existence. Despite his emphasis upon the importance of inwardness and abandoning materiality, Eckhart's mysticism is clearly "a mysticism of everyday life," to quote Bernard McGinn's famous dictum about Eckhart. [18]

For Eckhart, both emptiness and activity are necessary in our lives: both the freedom of detachment and what he calls "work and activity in time," which he says does not lessen eternal happiness and is even necessary to get to God.

In fact, he believes Martha is sufficiently mature to be able to work undisturbed in the midst of the world's busyness; a life like hers, much of it spent in the kitchen, can be a nobler communion with God than any except the highest unmediated vision.

Finally, one should also note not only Eckhart's apophatic unsaying of the substantialist deity but that part of it included his apophatic unsaying of gender essentialism.

MODERN SPIRITUALITY

Meister Eckhart has become a hero of modern spirituality,[19] and, in some respects, has inspired a kind of syncretism and search for similarities between Eastern and Western religions, drawing the attention of contemporary non-Christian mystics. His famous saying, "The Eye with which I see God is the same Eye with which God sees me,"[20] resonates as a contact point between these traditions and Christian mysticism.

Arthur Schopenhauer, the 19th-century German philosopher, explored comparisons of Eckhart's views with the teachings of Indian, Christian, and Islamic mystics and ascetics. Erich Fromm, the renowned 20th-century humanistic psychoanalyst and philosopher, helped renew awareness in Eckhart's teachings, drawing upon many of his themes in his own work. Eckhart inspired United Nations Secretary General Dag Hammarskjöld and his concept of spiritual growth through selfless service to humanity, expressed in his best-selling contemplative diary *Vägmärken* (*Markings*).[21]

American theologian Matthew Fox is a prominent proponent of the Creation Spirituality movement that builds on Eckhart, as well as on other mystics like Hildegard of Bingen, Francis of Assisi, Julian of Norwich, Dante Alighieri, and Nicholas of Cusa.[22]

Eckhart's theology provides the primary groundwork for creation-centered spirituality. Unlike traditional theologians, Eckhart believes that mystical union involves our moving back into the real-world pain that engulfs creation and society. Eckhart views this as a four-fold path (*via*, in Latin): (1) *Via Positiva* (awe and wonder), (2) *Via Negativa* (letting go and letting be), (3) *Via Creativa* (creativity, art, beauty, dance), and (4) *Via Transformativa* (compassion, justice-making).

Like Moses de León's understanding of the spinning, non-linear Tree of Life, described in the next chapter, Eckhart does not believe these paths form a straight line, but continuous spirals, interlocking with each other. The first path of *Via Positiva* is simply the mystic's sense; Eckhart believed every person has potential, celebrated in the awe and wonder of creation. As to *Via*

Negativa, Eckhart's idea of letting go, emptying, sinking is quite different from the "purgation" tradition of non-apophatic mysticism thinkers. His *Via Creativa* encompasses both illumination and union, but extends well beyond those with his idea that, when one births God, one also births creativity (creative action) in the world.

As with other apophatic mystics, like Jalal ad-Din Rumi and Moses de León, Eckhart's *Via Transformativa* is a reminder that the aim of the mystic journey is not just union itself, but compassion, justice-making, repairing the world, and filling it with love.[23]

Eckhart's theology, while deep and layered in metaphors of unsaying, is extremely simple. His mysticism "does not demand a lot of baggage for the journey, it demands no gurus, no fanciful methods other than the discipline that all art requires, not excessive exercises or retreats. This is why Eckhart can call his a 'wayless way' available to all, and also why he points out that 'she who has found this way needs no other.'"[24]

Meister Eckhart indeed is an icon of mystical spirituality, reaching and resonating across generations and centuries in a way of which other mystics could only dream—were this of concern to them.

NOTES

1. Eric Gilmour, "Bernard McGinn on Meister Eckhart," May 21, 2103, https://www.youtube.com/watch?v=eesLtg5ywrU.

2. Bernard McGinn, *The Mystical Thought of Meister Eckhart* (New York: Crossroad Publishing Company, 2001), 14.

3. Ted Nottingham, "The Secret to Divine Consolation by Meister Eckhart," April 7, 2014, https://www.youtube.com/watch?v=2VHnMkb0DAI.

4. See Nicholas of Cusa, *The Vision of God* (San Diego, CA: The Book Tree, 1999).

5. Martin Luther published an edition of Theologia Germanica in 1516. Luther said he owed more to it than to any book apart from the Bible and the writings of Augustine. It focuses on the "divine life," which is directed or led by the "true light" of God, and offers a substantial amount of insightful spiritual advice in plain language.

6. See "Meister Eckhart's Sermons," *Christian Classics Ethereal Library*, June 1, 2005, http://www.ccel.org/ccel/eckhart/sermons.toc.html (seven of his most important sermons).

7. Meister Eckhart, "The Nearness of the Kingdom," *LearnOutLoud*, Sept. 26, 2013, https://www.youtube.com/watch?v=StAoAqa08LM.

8. See Robert A. Jonas, "Bernard McGinn on Meister Eckhart (1260–1327, C.E.)" ("Mystical Language in Meister Eckhart)," Nov. 5, 2011, https://www.youtube.com/watch?v=Uxh2MHzEc3g.

9. Pseudo-Dionysius the Areopagite was a Christian theologian, philosopher, and mystic of the late 5th to early 6th centuries and author of the *Corpus Areopagiticum* (or *Corpus Dionysiacum*), mentioned earlier in Chapter 3.

10. Matthew Fox, *Meditations with Meister Eckhart* (Rochester, VT: Bear & Company, 1983), 88.

11. Meister Eckhart, *The Complete Mystical Works of Meister Eckhart*, trans. Maurice O'C Walshe (New York: Crossroad Publishing Company, 2010) (Sermon 1); Carsten Barwasser, "Meister Eckhart: The Birth of God in the Soul," March 1, 2014, https://www.youtube.com/watch?v=JBjiD7tvMEM.

12. The 16th-century Spanish mystic John of the Cross speaks of the "dark night of the soul." *See* Loreena McKennitt, Sept. 17, 2013, "Dark Night of the Soul," https://www.youtube.com/watch?v=fzHeT-Go4Zg (lyrics set to music).

13. Matthew 16:25.

14. Meister Eckhart, *The Complete Mystical Works of Meister Eckhart* (Sermons 13b, 4).

15. Ibid. (Talks of Instruction 1, 7).

16. Ibid. (Sermon 55).

17. Luke 10:38–42.

18. Bernard McGinn, *Meister Eckhart and the Beguine Mystics: Hadewijch of Brabant, Mechthild of Magdeburg, and Marguerite Porete* (London: Bloomsbury Publishing, 1997), 113.

19. See *The Eckhart Society*, http://www.eckhartsociety.org/.

20. Meister Eckhart, "Sermon IV: True Hearing," *Christian Classics Ethereal Library*, June 1, 2005, http://www.ccel.org/ccel/eckhart/sermons.vii.html.

21. See "Dag Hammarskjöld—biography," *Dag Hammarskjöld Foundation*, http://www.daghammarskjold.se/biography/; "Dag Hammarskjöld, "Quotes," Goodreads, https://www.goodreads.com/author/quotes/946904.Dag_Hammarskj_ld.

22. See Matthew Fox, *Breakthrough: Meister Eckhart's Creation Spirituality in New Translation* (Colorado Springs, CO; Image Books, 1980).

23. Fox, *Meditations with Meister Eckhart*, 3–7.

24. Ibid., 6–7.

Chapter Seven

Moses de León

No other love compares unto ecstasy of the moment,
when spirit cleaves to spirit and becomes one
— one love.

—*The Zohar*

Moses de León (Moses Ben Shem Tov) (1250–1305) was a Jewish rabbi of the Kabbalah tradition and author and publisher of the *Sefer ha-Zohar* (*Book of Splendor,* or *Radiance*), one of the most significant and foundational works of Jewish mysticism.

The Zohar is a masterpiece of Kabbalistic thought and tradition. For centuries, it rivaled the Hebrew Bible itself and the Talmud (the rabbinical compendium of law, lore, and commentary) for influence among Jews.[1] *The Zohar*'s authorship was in dispute for a while, but now is decidedly attributed to de León.

As with many Jewish mystics, much of Moses de León's life is unknown. He lived in Guadalajara until 1290, the Kabbalah center in Muslim Spain. After that, he traveled widely in al-Ándalus, eventually settling in Ávila, where he died.

Rabbi Lawrence Kushner has described Moses de León as ". . . gentle yet (we must assume) mischievous, world-renouncing but in love with things that smelled and tasted good. His eyes were always wide open, not glassy or penetrating, just wide awake as if he were always seeing things for the first time."[2]

De León was familiar with the philosophers of the Middle Ages and the literature of Jewish mysticism, including Isaac Ben Jacob Ha-Kohen's *Treatise on the Left Emanation*, which greatly influenced him. He knew and relied on the writings of Solomon ibn Gabirol, Yehuda ha-Levi, Moses Maimonides, and others. He also had some sort of relationship with King Alfonso X, the intellectual leader of a renaissance of sorts at the time. Alfonso was relatively tolerant of Muslims and Jews and apparently had an interest in *The Zohar* and Kabbalist notions.

Apart from religious study, de León was attracted to philosophical thought, including Maimonides' *Guide for the Perplexed*. Eventually moved by desire, however, to counteract the rationalistic trends of his day, he turned to the Kabbalah and immersed himself in its lore, while traveling among the Jewish communities of the region.

The Neoplatonism of Spanish mystics of the era also helped fashion his thought; and he is thought to have had a close friendship with Joseph Gikatilla, a Spanish Kabbalist and disciple of the renowned Abraham Abulafia, who developed elaborate contemplative techniques. In fact, Gikatilla's *Ginnat Egoz* (*Nut Orchard*) provides some of *The Zohar*'s key terms.

De Léon was a prodigious author. He wrote with homiletic brilliance, crafted eloquent phrases and striking poetic imagery, and created artful commentaries, with which to summon mystical experiences among his readers. However, he often credited earlier respected scholars and sages as authors of his works, most likely to give them greater authority than they would have under his own name. This was not an uncommon technique,[3] and one he employed with *The Zohar*, which led to some controversy of authorship.

De Léon designed his works to spread Kabbalah teachings, as he conceived them. Most of these writings were in Aramaic. De León also composed Hebrew pseudepigrapha (writings attributed to a respected author) on ethics and eschatology of the soul. He based his Hebrew writings on the same sources as those in *The Zohar*, and frequently made oblique references to it. These writings, in effect, are his exegesis of the doctrines in *The Zohar*.

THE ZOHAR

The Zohar has three parts, often published in five volumes: the *Book of Zohar* proper (*Book of Splendor*), the *Tiqqune Zohar* (*Restoration of Splendor*), and the *Zohar Hadash* (*New Zohar*). *The Zohar* in reality is a not a single book, but a complete body of literature, a kind of mystical novel or compendium, with its 2000 pages drawn together under a single title. It also apparently recounts various medieval legends, including ideas about Satan, demonic powers, and sorcery, as well as formulas to protect oneself from such evil influences.[4]

The Zohar, written mostly in an artificial, literary Aramaic, presents itself primarily as a series of mystical commentaries on the Torah (or Pentateuch), the Five Books of Moses, in a manner much like the traditional *midrashim*, or homilies based on Scripture. In *The Zohar*, Rabbi Shimon ben Yochai (also known as Rashbi), a legendary 2nd-century rabbi and miracle worker, and his disciples engage in a series of dialogs, against the backdrop of an imaginary Palestine, which reveal God manifested in a series of ten descending emanations or *sefirot* (such as God's love, God's beauty, God's sexuality, and God's kingdom). There is a startling eroticism about *The Zohar* that is common in many mystical writings.

As noted already, at one time there was controversy whether *The Zohar* was de León's original work or, as he claimed, work from ancient manuscripts, dating back to Shimon bar Yochai for which Moses de León was but a later-day scribe. Most authorities today solidly assign it to de León.

Gershom Scholem, a great 20th-century scholar of Jewish mysticism, vouched for de Léon's authorship as his struggle against the rise of rationalism among Spanish Jews and laxity in religious observance. It was an attempt to reassert the authority of traditional religion ("Kabbalah" itself means "receiving" or "tradition") by giving its doctrines and rituals a fresh, radical, and persuasive reinterpretation and ascribing it to an older, revered authority.

Using Shimon bar Yochai's name as a penname also gave de León "cover" and authority for introducing his radical ideas about God in *The Zohar*—a brilliant tactic.

On the issue of authorship, there is a narrative that, on a trip to Valladolid, de León met the Palestinian Kabbalist scholar Isaac ben Samuel of Acre, who wanted to see the centuries-old *Zohar* manuscript. De León said he had been circulating hand-made copies of it since the 1280s. De León promised to show it to him at his home in Ávila. Because *The Zohar* was ascribed to Shimon bar Yochai, such an original manuscript would have been invaluable. De León died a few months later, before he could fulfill his promise; and tradition has it that his widow denied the existence of the manuscript, claiming that de Léon himself was *The Zohar*'s author.[5]

Following his death, *The Zohar* continued to have enormous influence on the Jewish community throughout the following four centuries, stimulating great interest in mysticism. *The Zohar* expanded the Kabbalah from a few treatises or tracts into a vast work. *The Zohar* became not only a body of mystical wisdom associated with the Jewish community but influenced mystics of other traditions and had a presence in Renaissance literature and spirituality.

Indeed, *The Zohar* became popular with some Christians,[6] who believed it affirmed certain doctrines of theirs, such as the Trinity and humanity's Fall. By the 17th century, even a Christian Kabbalah literature had developed.

Many rabbis praised *The Zohar* for its opposition to religious formalism; and, because it encouraged people's imagination and emotions, it reinvigorated the spirituality of Jews who felt stifled by Talmudic scholasticism and legalism. For many Jews, *The Zohar*'s lyrical mystical concepts helped them understand and cope with the oppression that seemed their lot in life in societies dominated by other religious groups.

Some rabbis, however, were alarmed by what they deemed *The Zohar*'s superstitious and magical tendencies. Its appeal to the goal of mystical ecstasy, they feared, would produce unengaged, escapist spiritual romantics, instead of individuals involved with life's day-to-day needs.

Features of *The Zohar* eventually became part of the Jewish liturgy in the 16th and 17th centuries, and many Jewish poets of the era integrated its ideas and expressions into their work. Rabbi Yisrael ben Eliezer (also known as the Baal Shem Tov) and the movement of Hasidic Judaism in the 18th century, with its emphasis on mystical thought, revived interest in the Kabbalah and *The Zohar*. Today, *The Zohar* is once again widely read, though many non-Hasidic rabbis still look askance with suspicion.[7]

THE ZOHAR AND KABBALAH

Moses de Leon almost singlehandedly expanded the Kabbalah from a few treatises or tracts into the vast Zohar which hand enormous formative and historical impact on the Kabbalah.

The Kabbalah had begun to come together in the 12th century in Seville among traditional Jewish scholars, mystics, and lawyers. Unlike other Western traditions, in which personal testaments of mystical union predominate, the Kabbalah is both a tradition and a literature of communal wisdom.[8] There is not a single Kabbalah "manual" or book because so much of it is tradition.

The definition of Kabbalah varies according to different tendencies and traditions of those following it.[9] Although used by some Jewish denominations, Kabbalah is not itself a religious denomination. Kabbalah's followers consider it as a necessary part of the study of the Torah. Some Jews accept Kabbalah doctrines as the true meaning of Judaism, while others reject them as heresy and contrary to authentic Judaism.

The Kabbalah was likely first published in Provençe, France, in 1176, having spread there from the Middle East through northern Europe. It flourished in Muslim Spain and from there extended through the Mediterranean world, incorporating some Neoplatonic ideas that were taking on significance in Christian, Islamic, and Sufi mysticism.[10]

Until relatively recent times, the Kabbalah was a wisdom restricted to mature men, those with rabbinical learning and preferably married. Young men and women were excluded so as to "protect" them, for, like other mystical experiences, it was to embrace fire.

Basically, the Kabbalah is a set of unique mystical religious teachings to explain the relationship between an unchanging, eternal, and mysterious *Eyn Sof* ("no end") and the mortal and finite universe (God's creation). De León asked, "Is there ought present that is thinkable?" the answer is *Eyn* ("there is nought").[11]

The Kabbalah seeks to define the nature of the universe and the human being, the nature and purpose of existence, and various other questions. It presents methods toward understanding these concepts and thus attaining spiritual realization.

Kabbalists and Jewish mystics generally subscribe to the Pardes (or, PaRDeS) method of Torah study to help guide one toward the mystical experience. Pardes is an acronym of the Hebrew initials of the four steps of the study, which sometimes overlap: *Peshat* (plain reading of the text), *Remez* (an allegorical or figurative approach to the text, revealing a deeper meaning), *Derash* (a teaching or application of the first two steps, like a sermon, sometimes combining two unrelated texts), and *Sod* (the hidden, secret, or mystic meaning of a text, revealed through inspiration or revelation). Pardes exegesis is generally seen as having a mystical link to the Hebrew *pardes* ("orchard'), from which the English "paradise" has its origins. The Talmud uses *pardes* for both the Garden of Eden and its archetype in heaven.

The Kabbalah expresses it thus:

> When a person, by means of his studies, reaches the level at which he wants nothing but spiritual elevation and at which the person accepts only the bare necessities of life in order to sustain physical existence, not for pleasure's sake, this is the first step of that individual's ascent to the spiritual world.

Kabbalists see two aspects to God in the nature of the Divine: God in essence, absolutely transcendent, unknowable, limitless Divine simplicity; and God in manifestation, immanent, the revealed persona of God through which God creates, sustains, and relates to humankind.

Kabbalists speak of the first as *Eyn Sof* (meaning "the infinite," "the endless," or "the limitless"). Of the impersonal *Eyn Sof*, nothing can be grasped. It is much like the "nothingness" of "unsaying" or "nihil" for Meister Eckhart and "nada" for John of the Cross, although "unsaying" admits of no definitions since a definition by its nature creates finiteness.

The second aspect of God, the divine emanations are accessible to human perception, dynamically interacting throughout spiritual and physical existence. They reveal the Divine immanently, and are bound up in the life of people. Kabbalists believe the two aspects of God are not contradictory, but complement one another, revealing the concealed mystery from within the Godhead.[12]

A crucial characteristic of *The Zohar* is its ability to embrace, and even woo, paradox. *The Zohar* articulates a paradox of opposites—the masculine and feminine, the transcendent and immanent—and describes God in both masculine (*Elohim* or *YHWH*), and feminine language (*Shekhinah*),[13] radically challenging traditional notions of God, especially the view of God as male. The paradox is based on the principle that all visible things have an external, visible reality and an internal one, which hints at the reality of the spiritual world.

Both masculinity and femininity play a crucial, and even erotic, role in *The Zohar*'s vision of the Godhead (Godhood or God-ness, the state of being God); they are the divine twin souls, as it were. This femininity and masculinity comes into play in how de León describes the Tree of the Sefirot.

While God may appear to exhibit dual natures (masculine-feminine, compassionate-judgmental, creator-creation), adherents of Kabbalah have consistently stressed the ultimate unity of God and God as genderless. God's name likewise is genderless. Thus, in all discussions of the male and female attributes of God, the hidden nature of God exists above it all without limit, being called the Infinite or the "No End" (*Eyn Sof*)—neither one nor the other, transcending any definition.[14]

De León's understanding of the divine feminine, *Shekhinah*, was new to Judaism at the time. It was God's *presence* manifest, for example, in the Book of Exodus' cloud by day and fire by night that hovered over the tabernacle, which housed the tablets of the Ten Commandments.

Though God has no gender, there are masculine and feminine nouns that refer to different "sides" of God, the goal of which is to unite them back together so that they no longer exist in themselves, but only the genderless God.

One of the salient themes of the Kabbalah is the warning that, for their own comfort, people "corporealize" God or diminish God to limits set by the poverty of their spiritual imagination. It is a trap that destroys faith, which is meant to engage, and thus seek union with, God.

According to tradition, Kabbalah dates from Eden, originally transmitted orally as a discrete revelation to the *Tzadikim* (righteous people), preserved by the privileged few, such as the patriarchs, prophets, and sages, and eventually "interwoven" into Jewish religious writings and culture.

In the view of Kabbalah adherents, its origin begins with secrets that God revealed to Adam. For Kabbalists, the Torah's description of creation in the Book of Genesis reveals mysteries about God, the true nature of Adam and Eve, the Garden of Eden, the Tree of Knowledge of Good and Evil, and the Tree of Life, as well as the interaction of these supernatural entities with the Serpent, which leads to disaster when Adam and Eve eat the forbidden fruit.

Unlike Augustine's idea of the Fall, *The Zohar* does not subscribe to the idea that Adam's disobedience made the world or humanity evil. Rather, Adam and Eve simply introduced evil things into the world with the capacity, now as then, to separate us from union with God.

The account of Adam in the Garden for Kabbalists is not only about God (God's transcendent, masculine side, *Elohim* or *YHWH*) driving Adam from the Garden but also about Adam rejecting God and divorcing himself from God, thus causing God (God's immanent, feminine side, *Shekhinah*) to withdraw from the Garden and Adam and go into exile with Adam and then to "walk with" the human community to try to bring it back into union with the genderless God, obliterating the paradox of the "male" and "female" sides of God.

Professor Soltes writes that "The failure to adhere to God's commandment represents a failure to do good, not an act of *being* evil. Evil is therefore not a creation in and of itself but an arrival made possible by human failure to be good."[15] To fulfill the hope of again achieving that union, people must practice attachment to God by observing the commandments.

There are other events in the Torah that have taken in Jewish mystical interpretations, such as Moses' encounters with the burning bush and God on Mount Sinai, Ezekiel's visions in particular, Isaiah's temple vision, and Jacob's vision of the ladder to heaven.

Hasidic thought extends the Kabbalah's divine immanence by holding that God is all that really exists, all else being completely undifferentiated from God's perspective—a monistic panentheism. Accordingly, God's existence is "higher" than anything that this world can express or understand. Yet, God includes all things of this world within God's Divine reality in perfect unity, so that the creation effects no change in God at all.

"God is our sense of self," writes Rabbi Kushner,

> . . . our innermost essence, encountered throughout all creation. Our selves are made of God's Self. But this does not mean that the world is our creation, or that we are God. It does mean that this awareness, this sense of uniqueness we feel cannot possibly come just from ourselves. It is bigger than us and must be in everyone else. In all living things. In stones and water and fire. Everywhere. Indeed, this sense of self, this *Anochi,* is so holy we correctly intuit that it has created us.[16]

Kabbalistic thought gives humans the central role in Creation: their souls and bodies correspond to the supernal divine manifestations.[17] This view led to a profound spiritualization of Jewish practice and ritual. Kabbalistic thought highlighted and energized conservative Jewish observance. This is expressed in many fashions, including this attribution to Rabbi Hillel:

> Who is wise? The one who learns from all people . . . .
> Who is mighty? The one who subdues the evil inclination . . . .
> Who is rich? The one who rejoices in his or her portion . . . .
> Who is honored? The one who honors other human beings . . . .

Kabbalah teachings accorded the central role in spiritual creation to the traditional *mitzvot* (religious duties, practices, and observance), whether the practitioner of *mitzvot* was learned in Kabbalah knowledge or not. Pairing Jewish observance and worship with mystical intentions infused those rites with power. Thus, sincere observance by common folk, especially in the Hasidic popularization of Kabbalah, could replace esoteric mystical abilities, and help "reveal" the hidden God in creation. They could be "building blocks" of creation.

As Rabbi Abraham Isaac Kook (1865–1935), Kabbalist and renowned Torah scholar, expressed it:

> Therefore, the pure righteous do not complain of the dark, but increase the light; they do not complain of evil, but increase justice. They do not complain of heresy, but increase faith. They do not complain of ignorance, but increase wisdom.

One more point of interest: Kabbalistic belief expanded biblical and *midrashic* notions that God enacted Creation through the Hebrew language and through the Torah into a full linguistic mysticism. Thus, every Hebrew letter, word, number, and even accents on words of the Hebrew Bible contain esoteric meanings, describing the spiritual dimensions within exoteric ideas. Kabbalah teaches textual interpretation methods that help understand these meanings. Each letter in Hebrew also represents a number. Unlike other languages, Hebrew never developed a separate numerical system. By converting letters to numbers, Kabbalists could find hidden meaning in each word.

Sefirot

In the Kabbalah, the universe consists of a series of ten *sefirot* (emanations, personalities, or souls) of God, by which humans can gradually ascend toward a consciousness of the Divine through four stages of knowledge. Beyond the last stage, "knowledge through love," is the ecstatic state experienced by the great mystics through their visions of the Divine. This state is entered by quieting the mind and remaining motionless, with the head between the knees, absorbed in contemplation, while repeating prayers and hymns.

The *Zohar*'s *sefirot*, emanations, explain human destiny and God's commandments governing that destiny. Individuals can only partially understand these mysteries; but the *sefirot* form a "world of union," a mystical Tree of Life that communicates God's life to people and by which an individual can ascend to God in perfection. The present unredeemed condition of the world is due to impurity and evil that have ruptured the original union between God and God's *Shekhinah*, Presence.

In *The Zohar*, the *sefirot* are imaged with central, left, and right columns. As Professor Soltes explains, "The left is treated as male and active, and the right as female and passive—except that there is no left and right, male and female, active and passive in Godness."[18] The middle column thus represents harmony, and the ideal balance of divine justice and mercy.

One should not picture *The Zohar* tree in flat or limited dimensions, but imagine the interwoven nature of the tree and its dynamism. For Soltes, the best way to understand the Tree of the Sefirot is dynamically, spinning on an axis, centered in place in much the same way as the Sufi Whirling Dervish remains centered while spinning simultaneously. Thus, the categories of masculine-active-transcendent-dynamic and feminine-passive-immanent-static instantly collapse into each other "so that the one 'side' instantly becomes the other."[19]

It would be a mistake, though, to associate the tree with "aspects" of God only. The descending and ascending *sefirot* not only imagine "aspects" of God, but also God "as articulating the *process of creation,*" a downward emanation; the mystic "recapitulates" that process, channeling them "back" to the Creator. The mystic approaches the tree as dynamics of both "Climbing Jacob's Ladder" and "Dancing Sarah's Circle."[20]

The Zohar teaches that humanity's efforts toward moral perfection also can influence the spiritual world of the *sefirot*, divine emanations. People's practice of virtue actually can increase the outpouring of divine grace, causing God to act favorably (or reveal God's self more expansively). The opposite is also true, and helps explain evil in the world; humans divorce themselves from God through evil deeds, causing God not to act favorably and even to withdraw.

Later Developments

In the 16th century, Isaac Luria Ashkenazi (also known as "The Lion") (1534–1572) gave impetus for a new, systematized version of Kabbalistic thought that synthesized and expanded upon *The Zohar*. Luria was a leading rabbi and Jewish mystic in Safed in the Galilee region of Ottoman Palestine,[21] to where many Jews had migrated after expulsion from Spain. He is regarded as the father of contemporary Kabbalah.

Lurianic Kabbalah described new supra-rational doctrines of the origins of Creation and the cosmic role of each person in eschatological Messianic redemption.[22] This translated into emphasis on close kinship, ascetical practices, and communal-messianic rituals. Lurianic Kabbalah also opened up its teachings and contemplative practices to a wider community (albeit only men), believing that it would hasten redemption for the entire Jewish people. Paradoxically, the mysticism of Lurianic Kabbalah came to involve withdrawal from the larger community.

Teaching of classic Kabbalah texts and practice remained rather tradition-al in Judaism until recent times, handed down from master or teacher to disciple, and meditated upon by rabbinic scholars. However, this changed in the 20th century fairly dramatically, through deliberate reform and greater openness to, and desire for, Kabbalistic knowledge.[23]

CONCLUDING COMMENTS

In short, *The Zohar* re-imagines God in extraordinary ways. Humans can affect—and effect—God's actions; they nurture God or have the opposite effect. People's good deeds favorably affect and effect the flowing down of God's grace; and the reverse is true: humans can cause disorder in God by their bad deeds. By living a holy life, people actually make God present in the world in a real sense. God needs love, and people actualize God's divine potential in the world by keeping God's commandments: loving one's neigh-bor, helping poor persons, keeping the Sabbath, and so on. These concepts are not unlike those of many Sufi and Christian mystics.

Moses de León is one of history's most influential Jewish writers, ironi-cally much more so through the one work he published, not in his own name, but under the pseudonym of Shimon Bar Yochai. He breathed life into the Kabbalah, a breath so potent that it helped propel the Kabbalah through the centuries as a touchstone of Jewish mysticism.

We now return to the Taverna degli Alighieri in Venice and join the conversation with Jalal ad-Din Rumi, Meister Eckhart, and Moses de León.

NOTES

1. Probably the best version of *The Zohar* in English is the eight-volume set translated and prepared by Daniel C. Matt, with his excellent commentaries and notes, from 2003–2014: *The Zohar: Pritzker Edition* (Redwood City, CA: Stanford University Press, 2003–2014); and see PDF text, http://www.sup.org/zohar/.

2. Lawrence Kushner, *God was in this Place & I, i did not know: Finding Self, Spirituality and Ultimate Meaning* (GemStone Press, 1993), 132.

3. As noted earlier, another greatly influential mystical writer, Pseudo-Dionysius the Areo-pagite, probably a Christian theologian in Syria, wrote under the name of a famous convert of Paul, mentioned in the Acts of the Apostles. He actually lived in the late 5th and early 6th centuries.

4. The omni-eclectic travelogue style of *The Zohar* is reminiscent of Dante's *Divine Come-dy*, Chaucer's *Canterbury Tales*, and Cervantes' *Don Quixote*. Many consider Dante himself to be mystic; his work also considers the "eternal femininity" of God.

5. Andy Nastase, *"The Zohar:* Secrets of Kabbalah," *History Channel*, Feb. 12, 2014, https://www.youtube.com/watch?v=Xlx4QAjGfuw (exceptional overview of *The Zohar* and Kabbalah).

6. See, e.g., Billy Phillips, *Kabbalah Centre International*, Dec. 29, 2012," Kabbalah TV: Kabbalah and Christianity with Billy Phillips," https://www.youtube.com/watch?v=C-yxSGjOZDU .

7. See, e.g., *Kabballah Centre International*, July 11, 2006, "Power of Kabbalah," https://www.youtube.com/watch?v=OCRRSn96Ang; and Kabballah Centre International, http://kabbalah.com/.

8. Daniel C. Matt, *Rutgers*, Dec. 3, 2012, "Zohar and Kabbalah—Daniel Matt," https://www.youtube.com/watch?v=OAkCeMZk-Pw (outstanding hour-long, classroom presentation).

9. For a good overview and introduction, see Ron Feldman, *Fundamentals of Jewish Mysticism and Kabbalah* (Crossing Press Pocket Guides) (Berkeley, CA: Crossing Press, 1999); and Joseph Dan, *Kabbalah: A Very Short Introduction* (Oxford, UK: Oxford University Press, 2007).

10. John Kirvan, *God Hunger: Discovering the Mystic in All of Us* (Notre Dame, IN: Sorin Books, 1999), 140–41.

11. *Secret Garden: An Anthology in the Kabbalah*, ed. David Meltzer (Barrytown, NY: Barrytown/Station Hill Press, Inc., 2007), 157.

12. As noted earlier in the chapter about him, Meister Eckhart also draws a distinction between "Godhead" and "God," a divergence between the Unmanifest and Manifest Absolute.

13. Ori Z. Soltes, *Mysticism in Judaism, Christianity, and Islam: Searching for Oneness* (Lanham, MD: Rowman & Littlefield, 2009), 120–21.

14. *Secret Garden: An Anthology in the Kabbalah*, 157 ("There is no palpable existence whatsoever, either above or below, that does not proceed from the mystery of that one 'point.'").

15. Soltes, *Mysticism in Judaism, Christianity, and Islam*, 117.

16. Kushner, *God was in this Place & I, i did not know*, 147–48.

17. In the Christian Kabbalah, this scheme was often universalized to describe *harmonia mundi*, the harmony of Creation within humans. See Dan, *Kabbalah: A Very Short Introduction* (chapter on Christian mysticism).

18. Soltes, *Mysticism in Judaism, Christianity, and Islam*, 115.

19. Ibid.

20. Ibid.

21. Safed is considered one of Judaism's Four Holy Cities, along with Jerusalem, Hebron, and Tiberias, and a center of Kabbalah, Jewish mysticism.

22. See Gershom Scholem, *Kabbalah* (New York: Plume, 1995).

23. See Gershom Scholem, *Major Trends in Jewish Mysticism* (New York: Schocken Books, 1995).

Chapter Eight

The Conversation Continues, about the Divine

> No one can think of God . . . . Therefore it is my
> wish to leave everything that I can think of and
> choose for my love the thing that I cannot think.
> God may be loved but not thought. God can be
> taken and held by love but not by thought.
>
> *—Cloud of Unknowing*[1]

Eckhart: Well, now that dinner is over, we can try some of this delectable *cantuccini* that Rabbi Moses picked up in Florence on his way here and begin our long-anticipated conversation.

De León: I trust, Mevlana, you will not be offended if I sample some of the superb local wine; and Meister Eckhart, I notice, has brought along some excellent German beer. I know, as part of your religious practice, you do not drink alcoholic beverages.

Rumi: Not at all, Gentlemen; but thank you for asking. I am quite content with the tea. I certainly respect your choices, as you respect mine. Although we Muslins do not drink alcohol, we Sufis often use wine in metaphors for love. Bayazid Bastami, for example, an early Persian Sufi mystic, would be so intoxicated with the "wine" of God's presence that it transported him into ecstasy.[2]

De León: Thank you, Mevlana, for that insight. Before we begin, I have a short note, which my dear wife repeatedly instructed me to read. As you might have heard, she actually helped me prepare *The Zohar* in some respects, although, of course, I used Shimon Bar Yochai's name as its pseudonymous author.

Here is what she writes: "My dearest Moses, I want to caution you in your discussions to use as much inclusive language as possible. I know the challenge of this, of course, because so many mystics tend to speak of God as masculine, even though they know God has no gender; but my being a woman gives me special insight. And, if you don't . . . ." So ends her note, Friends.

Rumi: Ha, ha, Rabbi. Did she really write the note or is that another of your pseudonymous authors? You are known to be quite a character and playful in your meetings with others. But, in any regard, the point is well taken; and we will do our best.

Eckhart: Well, then, Friends, let us move on to our first topic, which is "God." I often put God in quotation marks because it is the god of our making, with all the human-created encumbrances and clutter with which we have surrounded God or the Divine.

As Descartes will say a few centuries hence, God made humans in God's image and likeness, and humans promptly returned the favor. This is to say, we have created a god of our limited understanding, reduced in description to an array of inadequate words that we can conjure up, however well-intentioned and seemingly well-expressed. In actuality, we cannot define God but only experience the Divine in what spiritual writers will call "mystical union," the melting away of the boundaries between human and divine, self and other.

This is to say, "God," as we humans might refer to the Divine in our limited understanding, is not the God of reality, the Source of Being. We cannot even use the word "reality" to describe either the Divine's transcendence or immanence: transcendence, meaning what we try to describe with words like "Creator" or "Supreme Being"; and "immanence," as the presence of the Divine everywhere and within everything, including within and a part of us, although always greater than any of us, or all of us.

I like how my Dominican colleague Thomas Aquinas, who had an apophatic streak in his theology, once expressed it; "God" is not a proper name, but a generic word from the German *got*, used for the generic Latin word *deus*. It may be that the more we see "God" as an appellation, the more difficult it is for us to approach and be in the mystery of the Divine. I am afraid, as time goes on into the centuries to come, "God" will become more of a proper name and people will lose the mystery that comes from the "un-naming" of God. One of the beauties of our era is the richness of creative expression that explodes forth from an un-named sense of the Divine.

Rumi: I greatly appreciate your commentary, Meister Eckhart, because my religious tradition, Islam, assigns the term "Allah" to the Supreme Being. This translates as "the God," rather than a name. In my own particular practice of Sufism, I talk about the "Beloved" as a more adequate expression of whom I am trying to convey through my poems and writings. Sufis often refer to the God as *al-Fattah* ("the Opening" or "Opener"), which is one of the ninety-nine names of Allah in the Qur'an.[3]

De León: This is an intriguing conversation. We in Judaism are not supposed even to attempt to pronounce the actual name of the Divine. We use a Hebrew tetragrammaton, four letters, for the sacred word, which transliterates into Roman script as YHWH ("Yahweh"). Indeed, we apply this technique to other languages. "G-d," for example, shows up in many Jewish English texts.

When we see YHWH written, we actually pronounce "Adonai" or "Lord" in its place. At one time, the sacred name could only be spoken once a year, and only by the high priest in the Holy of Holies. But that was before the Romans destroyed the temple. No one is totally sure of the word's origin; but it may derive from an old Semitic root, meaning "to be" or "to become," which actually would seem to fit well with our respective ideas of the Holy One.

This raises a thought-provoking question, Gentlemen; and I would be grateful for your learned comments. When we speak of "God," "divine love," "the Beloved," "Allah," and "Adonai" are we speaking of the same "person" or "entity"?

Eckhart: What a difficult query because it occurs to me the answer may be both "no" and "yes." "God," "divine love," "the Beloved," "Allah," and "Adonai" ("Yahweh") only become differentiated when we ascribe separate names to them. Once we do that, we have created discrete entities that we define distinctly, even if we assign similar characteristics to them, such as love and mercy, for example.

However, the "yes" part of this is that, once we do the "un-naming" and open ourselves to the Divine, then the divine is the Divine being born in us. Clearly, our respective religious traditions are, or should be, helpful to getting us to that point in our lives (although "that point" by definition is without definition).

De León: Since we are talking about "un-naming God" or "unsaying God," our colleague of the future, Professor Ori Soltes points to three passages from the Hebrew Scriptures that illustrate mysticism of unsaying: Moses' encounter with God on Mount Sinai, the call of Isaiah in the temple, and Ezekiel's vision of the heavens opening.

Let us explore the Moses example. Moses has three God encounters on the mountain. The first is before the burning bush; the second is when Moses receives instructions for the law; and the third occurs after Moses angrily smashes the original tablets of the Ten Commandments and returns to hew out another set. While each narrative reveals the intricate tension between transcendence and immanence, the third is illustrative.

When Moses returns to the mountaintop, he asks God to show him God's glory. Moses does not ask to look directly at God, but only to see God's glory,[4] for to see God's face is to die. God replies, "While my glory passes by, I will put you in a cleft of the rock, and I will cover you with my hand until I have passed by. Then, I will take away my hand; and you shall see my back; but my face shall not be seen."[5]

Our friend, Professor Soltes takes three insights from this account. First, even someone as great as Moses can only get so close to God. Not even a mystic with direct contact with God can ever fully behold the Divine. Second, God's description is not precise. The mystic cannot fully know God, but only God's glory. Since God is a being beyond being, as the Israelites believed, the language of "seeing" God's glory is metaphorical. And seeing only God's back implies that language totally fails in describing the holy. Third, the outcome of Moses' encounter with God is displayed across his countenance; his face shone because "he had been talking with God."[6]

Even though Moses could not look at God's face, the encounter radically transformed him into a new person. For those having a mystical experience, "the 'me' who returns to the *profanus* from the *mysterion* is not the same 'me' who sought it out . . . ."[7] By "profanus," he means everyday life on the other side of the veil, separating us from the Mystery.

Rumi: Thank you, Rabbi, for sharing these remarkable insights on the Moses narrative. It is very evocative and layered with much deeper meaning than one would take away from a first reading. Moses, in his mystical experience, encountered God as "nothing" or "no-thing" and returned to his community with a changed "face," no longer the Moses he once was.

Eckhart: As I was listening to you, Rabbi, it struck me that the text about Moses' God encounter is a perfect example of how language fails utterly in defining the sacred. One could argue this is precisely the acute difficulty of trying to conceptualize or explain the Christian mystery of the Trinity as "one in three and three in one."

As I see it, the Trinity means the Father birthing and loving the Son, the Word, as well as birthing the Son in us; and the Spirit as love joining them all so closely there is no division, but only total seamless unity in a way we cannot fathom it. The Trinity reflects the Godhead's eternal dynamism, which is even more potent when we "unsay" the term "eternal."

Any attempt to linguistically systematize a theology of the Trinity can quickly drift into what the scholars call "modalism" or even polytheism. This is why I pray "to God to rid me of God,"[8] to rid me of the constructs of God, made by religion, language, culture, and myself, that get in the way of a true relationship with God. For that reason, I am fond of using the metaphor that God is an infinite sphere whose center is everywhere and whose circumference is nowhere.[9]

As Professor Soltes will write, "language is a particularly rich and far-reaching instrument, but ultimately language falls short . . . . Words can hardly succeed in expressing the beauty of a sunset or the love [of] a parent for his or her child; how can they possibly afford an effective means of labeling or describing God . . . ?"[10] Even though this sense of the hidden is characteristic of all mysticism, it is particularly true of apophatic mysticism.

Rumi: We have something similar in Islam with the refusal to portray the Prophet Muhammad (peace be upon him) in an image. Even though the Prophet is not God, we see him as God's final and definitive prophet; and depicting his image (or any religious image, for that matter) is akin to reducing the sacred into a figure, an endeavor, which is always unsuccessful and human-limiting, bordering on blasphemous or even idolatry.

De León: We must always be on guard about limiting God, whether in language, thought, or theology. It is so easy to do that often we do not realize we are doing so.

Eckhart: Indeed, Rabbi Moses, quite so. Changing course a bit, I would note that my own religious tradition has no prescribed regime or single way for everyone to use to arrive at the point of meeting the Divine or, better, letting the Divine meet us. Of course, that then begs the question of preparing our way for the Divine with, or without, the help of a religious tradition.

I believe our nature is such that we are always seeking and searching for God, no matter what we are doing and no matter how often we might fall down in this quest. Those who go looking for God outside of themselves will fall short because we have to meet God, and God has to meet us, within ourselves.

We have to let God birth within ourselves. I call this birthing of the Word, the Son. This birthing of God can take place in every person, but it is only consummated in a person to the extent the individual strives toward virtuousness and then abandons the self to God. Life, justice, and equality come with the birthing of the Son.

It is in and through the deconstruction of self in detaching—letting go, relinquishing, unbecoming—that the birth of the Word takes place in the soul. The highest degree of the highest virtue is detachment. Detaching and birthing are not successive stages on the mystical journey, but flip-sides of the same coin.

Striving to eliminate what separates us from God is critical to allowing the birth of the Word, God. The striving is what is important. We cannot achieve the birth of the Word by ourselves. It has to come from God. It is God who births what I call the hidden Word, the Son, in the depth of one's being. We can open ourselves to this happening through receptiveness and passivity, through diminishing our ego-constructs; but it is God who births the Word in us.

When this happens, we become aware of it. In other words, we know that God is born in us when the mind is stilled and sense troubles us no longer; all things become simply God to us, for in all things we notice only God and God manifest in life, justice, and equality.[11]

Rumi: Certainly, part of emptying out ourselves is to become separated from earthly distractions and materialism and live simply. Our Sufi name comes from the word *suf*, which means wool. It was a name assigned to us because, in the beginning, Sufis wore simple brown wool garments, much like what Francis of Assisi, other mystics, and holy Christian people would wear five centuries later, to reflect a humble and detached lifestyle.

De León: Yes, Mevlana, humility and detachment are indispensable. All three of our religious mystical traditions have begun to adjust from emphasizing the inaccessible, transcendent awe of God toward experiencing the immanent love of God, and, through ascetical practice, opening ourselves to live in that love and share that love.

And, speaking of humility in another sense, I am always struck by the humility of God, that God wants to give the Godself away, instead of just enjoying the Godself. That is what love is about: giving yourself in love to another, and wanting to be loved by the other, which becomes a unity of lovers, a unity of love.

God loves us and created us, and wants nothing more than to be loved back and become one, One. The 19th-century mystical poet Francis Thompson, once lost to himself as a drug addict, will write a magnificent paean, describing God as the "Hound of Heaven,"[12] relentlessly pursuing us, even through the dark labyrinthine twists of our lives, so much does God love us and wants to be loved by us in return. The Lover wants passionately to be the beloved, to be one, One.

We, of course, have free will to say "yes" or "no"; and free will to move toward that union, if we desire. Moving toward that union means "cleaning house" so that we will have the passivity to let it happen to us, overtake us. This can happen for the agnostic as well, and perhaps for the atheist, too.

Eckhart: In my understanding, passivity is essential to the eternal birth within each of us. I am not talking about passivity as weakness, as I am sure none of us would propose in this context, but as inwardly emptying our mind and senses, to take "ourselves," our inauthentic self-construct, outside of ourselves, leaving nothing but the real self so that God may enter and unite with us.

Some mystics describe this experience as falling. The celebrated Jesuit priest Pierre Teilhard de Chardin, for example, in the 20th century will describe, almost hauntingly, his mid-life experience of falling into himself.

Pierre Teilhard de Chardin: Excuse me, Gentlemen. I heard mention of my name as if by summons from somewhere off in the distance; and suddenly I find myself here. But you all seem familiar. I think we already may have met in a different "place" at a different time; but I am pleased and honored to be here with you this evening, however briefly.

De León: Welcome, Père Pierre, my friend. So nice to see you again. Meister Eckhart was just beginning to relay a mystical experience of yours about "falling" that, I believe, you will describe in your book *The Divine Milieu*.

Teilhard de Chardin: Ah yes, truly astonishing and humbling! It happened during a period of meditation, and suddenly I had a profoundly gripping experience of falling, falling downward, past different "rungs" of personhood and individuality, ever deeper and deeper.

All the while, I was losing more and more contact with myself, until I finally landed in a darkness that was not me—an abyss, out of which flowed a current, which I dared call my self—not my various *personae* or self-constructs, but my authentic self.[13] It was, as you have analogized before, Meister Eckhart, like the mighty underground river of Being.

Deep in ourselves is an interiority or a "within"; it is an interiority that unites us all, the entire universe, God, and each other into one, One, as I think I heard you say, Rabbi. It is also the source of the essential dignity of each person and of the sacredness of creation. It is an interiority that merges contemplation and community activism, that unites the dueling duality that many spiritual writers have posited between contemplation and social activism—a great mistake in my view. This is a topic I am sure you learned masters will cover this evening.

Meister Eckhart, I must say I am struck by how your mystical writings and mine seem to coalesce in many ways. I would wager that your influence on me was deeper than I realized when I read some of your works.

Meister Eckhart: Thank you, Père Pierre; I am pleased, and humbled, to hear that perhaps God has been working through me.

Teilhard de Chardin: I came to understand profoundly that one's actions and passivities can be "divinized" by comprehending that the Son lies at the heart of the world which has brought one's being into existence, and which will bring it to fulfillment. One's being is not fulfilled in isolation, but in communion with God, the earth, and humanity, all together.

Meister Eckhart: Succinctly and eloquently expressed, Père Pierre.

Teilhard de Chardin: Thank you, Meister Eckhart. Your kind words honor me.

In any event, I truly wish I could stay longer, Gentlemen, and discuss this further. However, I hear a distant voice, gently beckoning me to depart your company and visit some friends in China where I once worked as a paleontologist. It is the same soft insistent voice that called me here to Venice. It has been a privilege to have visited with you for a brief respite and shared my modest thoughts.

Rumi: Thank you, Père Pierre, for your intervention and imparting your experience with us. We are appreciative that you found a way to preserve your writings, after church authorities ordered you not to publish, so that your books and essays would be circulated far and wide after your death. Your work, unifying the evolutionary materiality and consciousness of the universe into one, One, was extraordinary and insightful. You were clearly open to the Beloved's voice within you.

We bid you *adieu*. I am confident our paths will meet again. Take care.

Teilhard de Chardin: So long, Gentlemen. Good evening.

Eckhart: I wish Teilhard had been here a little longer. I did not have time to ask him if the rumors about the influence of *The Cloud of Unknowing* upon him were true. In any respect, his observations about his experience certainly show the importance of passivity and receptiveness in the spiritual journey.

Achieving true passivity is difficult and requires sustained effort. That means periods of temporary physical seclusion or retreat, perhaps several days, and the ability to expel ideas and thoughts banging around inside the head. This eventually will become part of centering prayer practice, which, I am sure, will come up a few times in our discussions: seclusion, a still body, and a quiet mind. "Listening" is the key, a consent to divine presence, moving from conversation to communion.

It also helps, as we have learned, to do centering prayer in a group, especially for the novice who must acquire some necessary skills; and ritual is likewise essential, such as bowing to each other or a periodic tap on a Tibetan singing bowl, followed by a short, deliberative processional walk and then returning to a seated position to "listen." This allows us to get fixed in God so that no one and no thing come between the individual and God. This is sometimes referred to as "standing in a mystery,"[14] "sacred pause,"[15] or popularized as "Hang up. Say hello." We are "activating" the Divine.

Rumi: This reminds me of what I tried to express in one of my poems:

> If the Beloved is everywhere,
> the lover is a veil;
> but when living itself becomes
> the Friend, lovers disappear.

De León: Mevlana, how beautiful! And, I recall that, like Meister Eckhart, you also have spoken of "going to the deep well of divine love inside each of us" and filling our jars there.

Rumi: Yes, thank you for remembering that. For us in Sufi Islamic mysticism, there is the lover, the loved one, and love. It is like a circle that keeps narrowing until the spiritual love binds the lover and loved one so close together that the three become one, indistinguishable from the other.

Eckhart: One could say that the mystic seeks God, which causes God to seek the mystic, and vice versa, until the boundary between lover and love, love and beloved, lover and beloved disappears, as you express it Mevlana. Lover and Beloved become each other or, as Professor Soltes will state it succinctly, "they are both *both*."

"Seeking" God, though, is not "striving for" God. "Seeking" means emptying oneself, moving away from the illusion of a separate self and into egoless clarity.

De León: You have a fairly evocative poem, Mevlana, which expresses this poignantly:

> One went to the door of the Beloved and knocked.
> A voice asked, "Who is there?"
> He answered, "It is I."
> The voice said, "There is no room for Me and Thee."
> The door was shut.
> After a year of solitude and deprivation, he returned and knocked.
> A voice from within asked, "Who is there?"
> The man said, "It is Thee."
> The door was opened for him.

Eckhart: Utterly marvelous, Mevlana. This reminds me of Jesus' words from the Book of Revelation. After advising people to repent and change their ways, he says: "Behold, I stand at the door and knock. If you hear me call and open the door, I will come in and sit down to supper side by side with you."[16]

Jesus also has a wisdom saying in the Gospel of Matthew, advising listeners to avoid gratuitous displays of prayer in public, and to pray privately in their inner room. Other than the obvious call to humility, we can make an analogy of that and interpret the "inner room" as the inner recess of our being where we let God be God.

De León: "Letting God be God" is key here. When we speak of the Divine, we need to be aware constantly of "unsaying" God, of not confining the Ineffable One to our language and images. God ultimately is "no-thing." We call this *Eyn Sof* ("no end") in the Kabbalah. I believe you use *nihil*, Latin for "nothing," Meister Eckhart. My future countryman and fellow mystic John of the Cross will use the Spanish word "nada."

We cannot even say that God is everything because the language implies a definition that is less than the totality and because there is always nothing to something and something can always be expanded. Learning how to experience God, rather than defining God, is what our kind of apophatic mysticism is all about.

Eckhart: Yes, Rabbi, I agree totally. God is nothing. No thing. God is nothingness; and yet God is something. God is neither this thing nor that thing that we can express. God is a being beyond all being: God is a beingless being.[17]

De León: The Kabbalah warns against "corporealizing" God, diminishing God with some human description, like the ancient white-bearded man seated on a golden throne high above cotton-like cumulus clouds, surrounded by

choirs of adoring angels. Doing so limits God to the poverty of our imagination. This becomes a trap that destroys the faith through which we must
engage with God.

· Having said that, I would note the paradox or irony of apophatic mystics
using language to describe their experience of the Divine. The very essence
of apophatic mysticism is to deconstruct or unsay the "essentialist" God,
such as God as the All-Knowing, the All-Powerful, the Infinite, and so on.
But then we turn around and use language to try express the Divine, albeit
much differently and allegorically, such as the feminine side of God, the
Lover, God being birthed as the Word of life, justice, and equality.

Of course, we have no choice but to use language to communicate what
we experience. The good part of this, though, is that it moves us into experiential modes that lead to union with God, not to doctrinal disputes, which
lead to division, thereby tending to fix the idea of separation from God—a
transcendent, judgmental God, instead of an immanent, loving God.

Rumi: Yes, this is not about creedal doctrines and theological syllogisms,
but about letting the sweet breath of the Lover carry us like a breeze into the
Lover's heart and melding us there as one in love's warmth. I empty myself
of my self so that God can flow into me and we become one.

De León: The Kabbalah is certainly strong in terms of describing direct
communication with God through the process of self-negation or "self-annihilation," as you frame it, Meister Eckhart. You and Marguerite Porete are
among the first Christian writers to use the term.

Rumi: This is another area of similarity among us. Many Sufis have the
same concept of self-annihilation, as well. Bayazid Bastami, the renowned
Sufi mystic of the 9th century, spoke of self-annihilation as the only state in
which a person could be in order to attain union with God.

Eckhart: This idea of self-annihilation or self-negation so that God can be
in us completely will lead scholars in the future to refer to us "panentheists."
It is a term taken from two Greek words meaning "God in everything" or
"everything in God." Another way of portraying this is that God interpene-
trates every part of existence, of which we are part, and timelessly extends
beyond it. Panentheism is much different from pantheism, which identifies
God as identical with the universe.

Unlike pantheism, panentheism maintains the identity and significance of
the non-Divine. It is essentially a combination of the concepts of theism (God
as the Supreme Being) and pantheism (God as everything). Panentheism
encompasses both the immanence and transcendence of the Divine.

Our 21st-century soul-mates, Professor Ori Soltes and Professor Michael
Sells, talk of a distinctive dialectic of transcendence and immanence in which
the utterly transcendent is revealed as utterly immanent. The goal of the
mystic is not to achieve unity with God but instead to achieve full transcognitive awareness of already being one with the One.[18]

De León: Yes, indeed. Mystical union brings a consciousness of the Oneness of everything. There is no dilemma of duality. The mystic receives a unifying vision of the One in the All and the All in the One.[19]

Meister Eckhart, you have expressed this idea brilliantly before: "The nearest thing one knows in God—for instance, if one could understand a flower as it has its being in God—this would be higher than the whole world."[20] And your flower maxim reminds me of a song lyric that Zebra will write: "How much more do you really think you know than a flower does about who is behind the door?"[21]

Rumi: What an elegant way to express it, as only a singer or poet can! I so much more prefer your flower aphorism to philosophical definitions, Meister Eckhart. Your flower has a living heart, the living heart of the Beloved. It is a classic mystical statement.

Eckhart: Thank you both, Mevlana and Rabbi Moses. If you do not mind, I would like to conclude this session with an earlier writing of mine that I think helps summarize mysticism, at least from my viewpoint, and which may share some common characteristics of what we three believe, especially the last part of the excerpt:

> For the power of the Holy Spirit seizes the very highest and purest, the spark of the soul, and carries it up in the flame of love . . . . The soul-spark is conveyed aloft into its source and is absorbed into God and is identified with God and is the spiritual light of God. There is in the soul something which is above the soul, Divine, simple, a pure nothing; rather nameless than named, unknown than known . . . . It is absolute and free from all names and all forms, just as God is free and absolute in [God]. It is higher than knowledge, higher than love, higher than grace. For in these there is still distinction. In this power, God blossoms and flourishes with all [the] Godhead; and the spirit flourishes in God.[22]

Yes, my dear Colleagues, we are each a spark, a flicker, of the Flame, just as those who have gone before us and will come after us are sparks, flickers, of the same Flame.

NOTES

1. *Cloud of Unknowing*, 6:130-31.
2. Rumi has a poem with similar sentiments:
   The moment we leap free of ourselves,
   the wine of the friend
   in all its brilliance and dazzle
   is held out to us.
3. "The Most Beautiful Names of Allah," *Threshold Society*, http://sufism.org/foundations/ninety-nine-names/the-most-beautiful-names-of-allah-2.
4. Exodus 33:18.
5. Exodus 33:22–23.

6. Exodus 34:29.

7. Ori Z. Soltes, *Mysticism in Judaism, Christianity, and Islam: Searching for Oneness* (Lanham, MD: Rowman & Littlefield, 2009), 98; Michael A. Sells, *Mystical Languages of Unsaying* (Chicago: University of Chicago, 1994), 24–25.

8. Reiner Schürmann, *Meister Eckhart* (Bloomington, IN: Indiana University Press, 1978), 219.

9. Meister Eckhart, quoted in Wayne Teasdale, *The Mystic Hours: A Daybook of Inspirational Wisdom and Devotion* (Novato, CA: New World Library, 2004), 189. Meister Eckhart, *Meister Eckhart: Teacher and Preacher*, ed. Bernard McGinn (Mahwah, NJ: Paulist Press, 1986), 75.

10. Ibid., 48.

11. Meister Eckhart, *The Complete Mystical Works of Meister Eckhart*, trans. Maurice O'C Walshe (New York: Crossroad Publishing Company, 2010) (Sermon 4).

12. "'The Hound of Heaven' by Francis Thompson," http://www.bartleby.com/236/239.html (Oxford Book of English Mystical Verse); see also Metrisch, Feb. 11, 2010, "Richard Burton reads the haunting poem 'The Hound of Heaven' by Francis Thompson," https://www.youtube.com/watch?v=gToj6SLWz8Q; Emblemmediallc, April 15, 2014, "'The Hound of Heaven': A Modern Adaptation," https://www.youtube.com/watch?v=RXlgz4aBKt8.

13. Pierre Teilhard de Chardin, *The Divine Milieu* (New York: Harper, 2001), 76 (complete text at https://archive.org/stream/TheDivineMilieu/The_Divine_Milieu#page/n0/mode/2up. See also Donald Goergen, "A Retreat with Pierre Teilhard de Chardin," *Now You Know Media*, https://www.nowyouknowmedia.com/a-retreat-with-teilhard-de-chardin.html (Conference 2).

14. See *Inward/Outward* (illustrated quotation) at http://inwardoutward.org/quote-author/doris-klein/ from Doris Klein. *Journey of the Soul* (Lanham, MD: Sheed & Ward, 2001).

15. See April Yamasaki, *Sacred Pauses: Spiritual Practices for Personal Renewal* (Harrisonburg, VA: Herald Press, 2013).

16. Revelation 3:20.

17. Matthew Fox, *Meditations with Meister Eckhart* (Rochester, VT: Bear & Company, 1983), 41.

18. Soltes, *Mysticism in Judaism, Christianity, and Islam*, 7.

19. F. C. Happold, *Mysticism* (New York: Penguin Books, 1970), 46–47.

20. Ibid.

21. Zebra, *Metrolyrics*, "Who's Behind the Door?" http://www.metrolyrics.com/whos-behind-the-door-lyrics-zebra.html.

22. Happold, *Mysticism*, 49.

Chapter Nine

More Tea, Wine, and Conversation

This Time, about Religion and Whether It Helps or Hinders

*We are in danger of withering from apathy,
of becoming empty reeds.*

—Hildegard of Bingen [1]

De León: Well, Gentlemen, that discussion about God leads us directly to our second topic of the evening, religion and whether it helps or impedes the mysticism quest. We can begin, now that kind innkeeper has brought your pot of postprandial *çay* tea, Mevlana, and our new bottles of wine and beer.

From my perspective, mystical tradition in Judaism, especially that of the Kabbalah, appears more influential and integrated into our religious practice than it is for Christians and Muslims; it is closely connected to the Torah, the first five books of the Hebrew Bible, sometimes called the Pentateuch. The Torah plays a central role in how we understand and practice our tradition.

In your case, Mevlana, I sense that the Islamic religious leaders more or less have a hands-off approach toward your brand of Sufi mysticism, although there have been, and will be, persecutions by fellow Muslims, to be sure.

Rumi: Yes, indeed, Rabbi, you are quite correct, unfortunately.

De León: As for the Christian religion, Meister Eckhart, one witnesses a severe tension between mysticism and church authorities. Indeed, toward the end of your life, the Archbishop of Cologne will drag you, of all people, a theologian, to trial as a heretic. You will lose and have to appeal to the pope to overturn the verdict. However, your untimely death will interrupt the dastardly process, which, in turn, ironically will help your future official "rehabilitation," though centuries later, alas.

Eckhart: Yes, the situation can be precarious if one runs afoul of the establishment. The hierarchs are so strong and tied to political power that they tolerate little deviation from the official line. Nor do they countenance any perceived challenge to their authority and sacerdotal role. I sometimes think they forget their function is to be God's messenger, not the message itself.

And the Inquisition is ever present, breathing down the necks of those about whom it receives complaints, no matter the motivation behind the charge. There often is a political reason for the persecution. In fact, it can even be internecine. Those who will prosecute me are of the Franciscan religious order and have become rivals of us Dominican friars. I am sure Francis of Assisi, himself a mystic, and founder of the Franciscans, would be horrified at this turn of events.

The ecclesiastical authorities have a troublesome time understanding, and probably instinctively fear, that the mystics' knowledge, like that of the prophets, especially apophatic mystics, is beyond normative knowledge. It is a kind of knowledge, as Professor Soltes will say, that connects mystics directly to the innermost, hidden recess of God, without the essential need of intermediary clergy. They certainly challenge the status quo and cause more than a little discomfort for the established order—a sharp thorn in its side.

De León: This raises the larger question of how religion can be manipulated, for whatever reason, such that it loses its mission of moving people toward union with the Divine. Indeed, it even subverts that spiritual journey for large numbers of believers and adherents. Some of the reason, no doubt, involves issues of control; bureaucracies and institutions inevitably make self-preservation and advancement their highest priority, and lose sight of their mission. Then, there is the matter of personal insecurity in the face of the unknown, and the Unknown. The situation becomes worse exponentially when there is no separation of religion and state.

The great rabbi, Jewish theologian, and social activist, Abraham Joshua Heschel, of the 20th century, will summarize it quite powerfully:

> Religion becomes sinful when it begins to advocate the segregation of God, to forget that the true sanctuary has no walls. Religion has always suffered from the tendency to become an end in itself, to seclude the holy, to become parochial, self-indulgent, self-seeking, as if the task were not to ennoble human nature but to enhance the power and beauty of its institutions or to enlarge the body of doctrines. It has often done more to canonize prejudices than to wrestle for truth, to petrify the sacred than to sanctify the secular. Yet the task of religion is to be a challenge to the stabilization of values. [2]

Eckhart: Yes, indeed. If religion only leads us around the edges of the Mystery, but not into the Mystery, then it fails in its purpose. Static creedal doctrines undermine the dynamic love of God and create the fiction there is only one well from the Underground River.

Rumi: According to my fellow Sufi, Ibn al-'Arabi, a mystic, whom we call the greatest master and the "Reviver of Religion": "Each person is oriented toward a quest for [one's] personal invisible guide, or . . . entrusts [one's] self to the collective, magisterial authority as the intermediary between [one]self and Revelation."

Ibn al-'Arabi taught Jews, Muslims, and Christians, and studied the Kabbalah and Torah. He respected diverse paths, had a universal and openhearted sense, and was fond of pointing out that the Qur'an says, "Wherever one turns, there is the Face of God." I believe, as he, that God is to be found everywhere and that we should always emphasize love over law. And religion should point us in that direction, and in no other. Mysticism is not about what we rationalize about God or theology; it is participation.

De León: My dear Mevlana, so well said! I am reminded of two often quoted passages of yours that are stirring and to the point:

> . . . I go into the Muslim mosque
> and the Jewish synagogue,
> and the Christian church,
> and I see one altar.
>
> . . . .
>
> Not Christian or Jew or Muslim, not Hindu,
> Buddhist, Sufi, or Zen. Not any religion
> or cultural system. I am not from the East
> or the West, not out of the ocean or up
> from the ground, not natural or ethereal; not
> composed of elements at all. I do not exist,
> am not an entity in this world or the next,
> did not descend from Adam and Eve or any
> origin story. My place is placeless, a trace
> of the traceless. Neither body nor soul.
> I belong to the Beloved, have seen the two
> worlds as one and that one call to and know,
> first, last, outer, inner, only that
> breath-breathing human being. [3]

Rumi: Yes! Thank you, Rabbi Moses. But, as I have often said, there are many times when I actually do not feel like I am "writing" my poetry, but rather "channeling" it.

I profoundly believe that, if religion gets in the way of entering into the mystery of Love, it must be ignored. Intellectual knowledge about religion cannot become religion itself. Religion is an intermediary, not the end goal.

The right practice of religion should help move us unto the Lover's embrace. Religion has to be transformative, transformative of ourselves and of the community, not something that emphasizes loyalty to a group or that claims superiority over all other groups. Religion must be a garden of life, not a citadel of exclusivity. One of my colleagues in Konya often reminds me of an earlier saying of mine: "Whatever purifies you is the correct road. I will try not to define it."

Eckhart: You say it superbly, Mevlana. I also believe that a religious tradition, with its rites, practices, teachings, and culture can be immeasurably important, and perhaps critical, in helping individuals break with their personal fetters and find union with God. Religious tradition has enormous potential in providing the grounding needed from which the person can move in the direction of the Divine.

We have noticed this happen with so many mystics, who thrive and grow within their traditions, even in the face of opposition. That, in turn, allows them to use the myth structure with which they are familiar to communicate their spiritual journey to others of similar religious and cultural backgrounds and thus encourage others on the path to the Divine. I use "myth" in its classic sense, as a narrative of underlying reality that we experience but cannot totally explain rationally. Myth, in this sense, is a poetic expression of life's underlying realities.

De León: Indeed, I agree. Our religious traditions may be useful as a guide to help us get to where and when we take the next step, from religious tradition, into being ready for union with God or whatever we want to name the Divine. We know, however, that we eventually have to un-name it, and be enfolded within its power, or within its love, that has no name or description.

Religion is not a goal in and of itself, as we have said fairly firmly, but a vehicle. Many people in the 21st century find serious flaws in formalized religion, and quite justifiably so. But sometimes I think that is because they only look at its veneer and do not dive into its deeper mystery and mythic narrative. The veneer is skin deep; the mystery and myth are heart deep.

Eckhart: For me, this conjures up the idea of a continuum that stretches from the unavoidable human flaw inherent in trying to understand the ineffability of the Divine to the outright control with which some religious institutions try to take over people's lives. Group-loyalty trumps God-loyalty. Beyond this pole, of course, lies the danger of extremism.

God's love is not exclusive and doctrinaire; nor should religion be. Killing people in the name of God, or causing them to suffer unless they convert, or consigning them to the fires of Hell is not the work of God. This is all abhorrent to God and prevents God's self-manifestation in the human community. How often have we sinned against God in the name of God?

All religious traditions suffer serious misadventures, defects, and maladies, historical and current; and we must call them out for what they are. However, to the extent we can put those flaws, and structural and organizational defects behind us or help reform them, and draw from the richness of the narrative, myth, and practices of our religious culture, we can find great assistance in our spiritual journey. Religion should strengthen who we are, not the reverse.

De León: Sometimes, there is a tendency to move from one religious tradition to another in hope of finding a "better" one. That may work for some, but not always.[4] Often it is better to rely upon the one most familiar to us, using that religious tradition as a guidepost along the footpath or directional arrow toward that inevitable horizon past organized religion. You penned a succinct verse about this, Mevlana: "You wander from room to room, hunting for the diamond necklace that is already around your neck."

This, in turn, prompted my memory of an insightful remark the Dalai Lama will make in the 20th century:

> I think it is usually better not to change [one's religion of origin]. The more we understand each other's ways, however, the more we can learn from each other. Our presentation of love and compassion may differ, but the concept of compassion remains the same. Once we realize this, and appreciate its deeper implications, it automatically brings genuine respect for other religions. And respect acts as a foundation for the development of harmony between different religious traditions.[5]

Rumi: What an excellent observation from the Dalai Lama, and right to the point! As our friend Wayne Teasdale, the Christian monk, will point out in the future, and which is good always to keep in mind: "the mystical tradition, which underpins all genuine faith, is the living source of all religion itself . . . . existence is a summons to the eternal journey of the sage, the sage we all are, if only we could see."[6]

Following through with Brother Teasdale's point that mystical experience gives rise to religion, in each of our Abrahamic traditions, our Scriptures are the starting point. They generally either record someone's mystical experience or foster a way of life related to the experience (Moses' law for example). We share some of the same Scriptures, but not all. So, it makes sense that, while we are each grounded in our use of the Scriptures, we should be open to others' use and understanding of them. Sometimes, it seems that our "political" egos get in the way of this sharing of spirituality. True holiness sees the Divine Lover everywhere, calling us to be open, and open ourselves to others.

De León: I always have found it personally helpful in my own personal journey to keep in front of my mind that religion, like education and schooling, is an institution that carries along insights, traditions, and knowledge from ages past and accumulates more as time goes on, from which we can benefit and grow. I can ignore or discard that which is not personally helpful or "take the good stuff, and leave the rest," as they say. Like education, religion is a social organization that brings, or should bring, to us the wisdom of others. In this case, it is wisdom about finding union with God.

It is always a challenge to find a spiritually nourishing community, for those who have none or may be thinking about looking for one; but it is worth the search. I, for one, do not want to sound the call that people should return to their church, synagogue, or mosque, just for the sake of returning. Not for a minute.

And, when I speak of a community, I am not talking about one of those "feel good" religious groups. It must be a community that challenges me spiritually, nurtures me, and provides the solid support I need on my journey, and which I, in turn, give to others in the religious community and the larger society.

Eckhart: I totally agree. Unless religion gives us a taste for, and of, God, it will lead us to become weary in our search within for God.

Rumi : There are many religious traditions, many significantly different from each other; but they all point in the same direction, toward loving union with the Beloved and with the community. We Sufis have a saying, "Our paths may not be the same, but our future is"; and then there is that picturesque metaphor "the moon shines on all corners of the world."

There are as many different paths to God as there are religions, and even a great diversity within a single religion. Of course, some find mystical union without any religious tradition at all. I have used a light metaphor before: the lamps are different but the Light is the same! The Divine Beloved pursues us all from wherever we are on our spiritual journey. [7]

Eckhart: You know, Mevlana, I have become a fan of your poetry. Sometimes, when I read or hear it, I feel like a bird being released from her cage and soaring gracefully into the blue sky. You have a poem in particular, "One Song," that speaks eloquently to religious diversity:

> Every war and every conflict between human beings
> has happened because of some disagreement about names.
> It is such an unnecessary foolishness,
> because just beyond the arguing
> there is a long table of companionship,
> set and waiting for us to sit down.
> What is praised is one, so the praise is one too,
> many jugs being poured into a huge basin.
> All religions, all this singing, one song.
> The differences are just illusion and vanity.
> Sunlight looks a little different on this wall
> than it does on that wall

and a lot different on this other one,
but it is still one light.
We have borrowed these clothes,
these time-and-space personalities,
from a light, and when we praise,
we are pouring them back in. [8]

De León: Thank you, Meister Eckhart, for reciting this marvelous poem of Mevlana.

Rumi: I think one benefit from a religious tradition that may be helpful is the practice of ritual. There is ritual in what we sometimes call a sacred space, such as church, mosque, or synagogue; and there is also ritual in culture, especially for special occasions marking a life transition (like birth, becoming an adult, marriage, death).

Ritual is an expressive endeavor, which our forebears have handed down to us, just as we, in turn, pass it on, perhaps somewhat modified. Ritual tries to express part of the Mystery that we cannot adequately articulate in our own words or practices. Ritual is a practice of the heart, not an exercise of the mind. It can be both a system of discipline and a source of refreshment, especially when adapted to current times and culture. [9]

Eckhart: Indeed, Mevlana. Your comment reminds me of religious historian Mircea Eliade's future and fascinating observation that all ancient cultures practiced rituals, which represented movement from the profane (nonsacred) to the sacred and in which an individual becomes detached "from profane time and magically re-enters the Great Time, the sacred time." [10] Myths and rituals of indigenous communities, which provided the foundational rhythm for modern religion, created the experience of what Eliade will call the "eternal return," stepping temporarily out of ordinary time and into "sacred time."

Rumi: Yes, Meister Eckhart, you have made a worthy reflection. Thank you for your intervention. That fits perfectly with our practice as Sufis. We have developed, for example, as part of our ritual, the mystical dance of whirling dervishes, expressing our union with the Divine and the Beloved's relation with all humanity, spinning, as it were, between heaven and earth. It is also a community dance, one in which we find companionship on our journey and provide companionship to others for their journey.

De León: What an illuminating example of ritual, Mevlana. Expressing the heart is essential to our spiritual journey. We Jews, for example, dance a lot, especially together as a group. It is part of our cultural rituals, which are related, of course, to our religion.

As you point out, Mevlana, there is something expressively spiritual that takes place in that sacred time, something that does not always happen with words alone. It also occurs as a community; it is greater than just an individual practicing ritual alone. Sometimes, it is strength that we give to each other, and strength that we receive from each other. Sometimes, it is joy or just a celebration of being with each other.

Eckhart: Ritual is important to us Christians as well. We have a great number of ritual practices. Many are formal church rites or ceremonies; but there also are many personal, informal rituals that Christians observe in their everyday lives. For us, because of our belief that Jesus was God Incarnate, we see, and seek, a more incarnational ceremonial experience of the One in our sacred time, that, through ritual, God becomes present among us in a different way.

The emphasis on community ritual prayer and its practice, and their interpretation, will change in different degrees with the movements that arise as part of the Protestant Reformation; but there always will be a community component and dynamic at play.

In any regard, I have been struck over the years how "packed" ritual prayer and tradition are. In other words, the closer God moves into union with us as we mature spiritually, ritual often takes on different and deeper meaning, quite distinct from what we originally understood.

Spirituality writers sometimes call this kind of prayer *kataphatic*, from the Greek word meaning "with form or images." It is prayer that has content; it uses words, images, symbols, and ideas. Sometimes people stop here in their spiritual practice, and go no further in their lives.

Others go on to mysticism from there, or on their own, to what is called *apophatic* contemplation, which means emptying the mind of words and ideas and simply resting in the presence of God. It is a common Eastern style to enable inward contemplation. Centering prayer is apophatic.[11] It is an emptying out, a listening.

One of your poems, Mevlana, expresses this well for me:

> Now be silent.
> Let the One who creates the words speak.
> He made the door.
> He made the lock.
> He also made the key.[12]

The apophatic tradition of mysticism focuses on a spontaneous or cultivated individual experience of the Divine beyond the realm of ordinary perception, an experience often unmediated by the structures of traditional organized religion. But this union with the Divine should also bring us into deeper union with the community since the Divine is present in us all.

De León: Quite so. But, if we're not careful, religious ritual can become rote, empty, or even magical. By "magical," I mean we think praying the words or doing the religious action will cause divine intervention on our behalf. That idea, of course, upends mysticism so that, instead of opening ourselves to the Mystery and wherever the Mystery takes us, we try to bend God to our will, not our will to God.

In fact, Mevlana, you have an awe-inspiring poem on this point that I often read in the morning before I begin my meditations:

> Pray the prayer that is the essence
> of every ritual. *God, I have no hope.*
> *I am torn to shreds. You are my first,*
> *my last and only refuge.*
> Do not do daily prayers like a bird
> pecking its head up and down.
> Prayer is an egg.
> Hatch out
> the total helplessness inside.

Eckhart: Such beautiful words, Mevlana; and thank you for sharing them, Rabbi Moses.

The one thing I would add to this discussion, Gentlemen, is that, whether or not one draws upon elements of her or his religious tradition for mystical practices, it is helpful for an individual to develop one's own personal ritual practices, such as entering into contemplation at a certain period of the day. It is good to have a designated "sacred space" where the person consciously enters and customarily occupies (such as a special chair), simply to *be*.

Another example of a personal ritual practice is to adopt a single-word mantra to help keep focus and draw us back when the mind begins to stray with distraction. I have always found it helpful to light a candle and offer words of praise to God at the beginning of my meditation, and then thoughts of gratitude when I blow out the candle at the end.

Sometimes, people use prayer beads or rosaries and recite repetitive prayers or mantras to help keep them focused from distractions during "free time" in their daily routines.

I would also urge an individual pursuing the mystical path to search out like-minded persons so that they could practice a community ritual as well. Personal and community rituals, in my view, are essential to each other. Strengthening one's relationship with the Divine entails strengthening one's relationship with the community, and vice versa. It is the Divine that unites us and draws us into the Mystery.

De León: My last comment for this part of our conversation would be to note the role of apophatic mystics with respect to their religious tradition. Mystics may find a struggle between their unremitting effort to "unsay" and what their tradition takes as its present reality or "says," such as defining God, or assigning certain attributes to God that do not reflect the fullest embrace of God. If taken positively and seriously, the mystic's critiques introduce a process of self-criticism to the community, which would strengthen the community. I think mystics owe it to their religious community to make this effort, if possible. But, if authorities reject this process, the tradition or community may eventually become a center of domination, exclusion, and power manipulation.

Eckhart: Indeed, Rabbi, I wholeheartedly agree. Religious communities will not change on their own without prompting and that is often what the mystics provide. Moses was a good example of this, and we see such prompting in our own time across all three of our spiritual traditions.

Rumi: Very good, Friends. Excellent conversation! Let us pause a moment, order refreshments, and then move on to our next topic. And let us conclude by recalling the graceful future words of Albert Einstein, physicist and 1921 Nobel Prize winner:

> The most beautiful and most profound emotion we can experience is the sensation of the mystical. It is the sower of all true science. [The person] to whom this emotion is a stranger, who can no longer wonder and stand rapt in awe, is as good as dead. To know that what is impenetrable to us really exists, manifesting itself as the highest wisdom and the most radiant beauty, which our dull faculties can comprehend only in their most primitive forms—this knowledge, this feeling is at the center of true religiousness. [13]

NOTES

1. Rumi also uses a reed analogy, talking of a reed longing to return to the reed bed, at the beginning of his *Masnavi*. See "Translations and Versions of 'The Song of the Reed' (*Masnavi*, Book 1: Lines 1–34)," *Dar-Al-Masnavi of the Mevlevi Order*, http://www.dar-al-masnavi.org/reedsong.html.

2. Abraham Joshua Heschel, *God in Search of Man: A Philosophy of Judaism* (New York: Farrar, Straus and Giroux, 1976), 414.

3. Ori Soltes notes that this poem and the preceding segment, although not found in the *Masnavi* or *Divan-e Shams-e Tabrizi*, have long been ascribed to Rumi and are validated, among other reasons, by the large number of unequivocally attributed passages, conveying the same thoughts. Ori Z. Soltes, *Embracing the World: Fethullah Gülen's Thought and Its Relationship to Jalaluddin Rumi and Others* (Clifton, NJ: Tughra Books, 2013), 34 n. 58. See IshqDaFakeer, July 1, 2008, "Rumi—Only Breath (Heart touching poem)," https://www.youtube.com/watch?v=L8hrF2CGTWY.

4. Ronald L. Grimes, *Marrying & Burying: Rites of Passage in a Man's Life* (Westview Press: Boulder-San Francisco-Oxford, 1995), 63 ("We cannot just decide to put the stuff down and walk off from it. We remain whatever we are—Canadian, American, Christian, Jewish, female, male, black, white, married, lesbian, domesticated, militaristic, consumerist. Though we [may] convert [to another faith tradition], we remain the same.").

5. *The Essential Mystics: The Soul's Journey into Truth*, ed. Andrew Harvey (San Francisco: HarperSanFrancisco, 1996), xxi.

6. Wayne Teasdale, *The Mystic Heart: Discovering a Universal Spirituality in the World's Religions* (Novato, CA: New World Library, 2001), 11, 3.

7. For a modern-day version of this teaching of Rumi, *see* Ori Soltes, Rumi Forum, May 16, 2013, "The Importance of the Rumi Forum," https://www.youtube.com/watch?v=zpfuFUjE9FI.

8. Coleman Barks, *Huffington Post*, Nov. 2, 2010, "Rumi's Poetry: 'All Religions, All This Singing, One Song,'" http://www.huffingtonpost.com/coleman-barks/rumi-and-some-new-ways-to_b_777382.html.

9. See, e.g., Tom F. Driver, *Liberating Rites: Understanding the Transformative Power of Ritual* (Charleston, SC: BookSurge Publishing, 2006) and *The Magic of Ritual: Our Need for Liberating Rites That Transform Our Lives and Our Communities* (San Francisco: HarperSan-Francisco, 1992).

10. Mircea Eliade, *Myths, Dreams, and Mysteries: The Encounter between Contemporary Faiths and Archaic Realities,* trans. Philip Mairet (New York: Harper & Row, 1975), 23.

11. For three excellent resources from the Contemplative Network, see "Judeo-Christian Prayer," http://www.contemplative.net/judeo-christian-prayer-t-6_33.html (written guidelines); "Judeo-Christian Contemplative Video," http://www.contemplative.net/judeo-christian-con-templative-video-a-48.html (five different video presentations); and "Prayer with the Songs of Taizé," http://www.contemplative.net/prayer-with-songs-taize-t-1_43.html.

12. Coleman Barks, a respected dramatic interpreter of Rumi's works, frames it thus: "Be loyal to your daily practice. Keep working. And keep knocking on the door. As you'll remember, it is said in one of Rumi's most pithy moments that the door we're knocking on opens from the inside."

13. Albert Einstein, quoted in Lincoln Barnett, *The Universe and Dr. Einstein* (New York: Bantam Books, 1979), 108.

Chapter Ten

Still More *Çay* and Conversation

*The Mystic, Society, and Justice—
and How They Fit Together*

When we arrive in heaven,
we shall find that everything
is held for the good
of all in common.

—Mechthild of Magdeburg

De León: Ah, how nice of the tavern owner to send over a pot of this new tea from the Orient, sweetened with delicious honeycomb, and hot buttered biscuits with cinnamon. We will be connoisseurs of tea before the morning arrives, I suspect. A good prelude to our moving into a discussion of mysticism and community.

You know, Meister Eckhart and Mevlana, I am always surprised with the stereotype most people have of mysticism, that it is practiced only by cloistered men or women, living in a much restricted environment and routine, silent and meditative, removed from the distractions of daily life. Perhaps even out in the remote desert.

But that is simply not the case or what it should be. Mystical experience and living should, and can be part of every person's life—and a joyous part, at that. In fact, and I know we all agree on this: true mystical experience flows over into helping make the community better and bringing justice to all people. Mystics profoundly realize that their own spirituality is part of something larger. Mystical experience without community involvement is, as Macbeth will say, "full of sound and fury, signifying nothing."[1]

Eckhart: Well, Rabbi Moses, I think you are absolutely right. Despite what earlier Christian giants like Augustine, Gregory, Bernard, and Benedict contended, I firmly oppose the idea that active community life and contemplative life are somehow opposed or antagonistic to each other, or, indeed, even irreconcilable. To the contrary.

Mystical experience should lead to community involvement, and there must be a deep spirituality within the active life. As Trappist monk Thomas Merton will write in the 20th century, an active life for justice without spirituality will quickly burn out.[2] One cannot work for a more just society without being spiritually grounded, which, for me, means being in close relationship or union with the Divine. There are other traditions of spirituality, of course, that sustain justice work; I am speaking from mine, as a Christian.

I caused a stir when I reinterpreted the story of Martha and Mary in Luke's Gospel. The common interpretation was that Luke appeared to paint Mary, sitting at the feet of Jesus, contemplative, in a better position than Martha, who was stressed with having to do all the work by herself and complained to Jesus that Mary was not helping. Jesus essentially replies, "Do not stress out. Let her be. She is doing the better thing."

Traditional theologians sometimes pointed to this story as Jesus affirming a dichotomy between the contemplative life and the active life and that the contemplative was superior. However, I turned the tables in a sense and tried to do away with the perceived irreconcilable difference between the two. I actually held up Martha as a model who could integrate a contemplative and active life, in a way that Mary could not yet do at the time.

Indeed, if we were to interpret the story as Martha calling Mary to a fuller life, to put her contemplation into practice, then we could understand Jesus' response as "Patience, Martha; she will get there. She is on the right track."

In fact, Teresa of Ávila, who will come after us in the 1500's, will write a meditation on Martha and Mary, that the unity of Martha and Mary in an individual is the goal of Christian life: "To give our Lord a perfect hospitality, Mary and Martha must combine."[3] Another mystic, Catherine of Siena will speak of a revelation that we are to walk on the "two feet" of love of God and neighbor.[4]

Indeed, the Birth of the Word happens in our everyday life, begotten as life, justice, and equality, and happens to all people of every tradition who open themselves to the eternal Birth of God in their soul.

Rumi: Yes, Meister Eckhart, your interpretation of this Gospel story fits better with my understanding as well. If the Divine Beloved is generous with us and seeks union with us, so too does the Beloved seek the same with everyone else—to love and be loved. That means we have to work for the fuller revelation of the Beloved in others, which, in turn, will be a fuller revelation for, and in, each of us.

Mohandas Gandhi, the 20th-century architect and philosopher of non-violent action and an admirer of Jesus and the Prophet Muhammad (peace be upon them), will be fond of saying that the best way to find yourself is to lose yourself in the service of others and that, if you don't find God in the next person you meet, it is a waste of time looking further for God.[5]

Eckhart: Interestingly, Rabbi Rami Shapiro in the 21st century will talk of each of us being assigned an angel, not to protect us, but to walk three or four feet in front of us, proclaiming, "Behold, here comes the image and likeness of God."[6]

Rumi: What an awesome thought of Rabbi Shapiro, Meister Eckhart! And Thomas Merton will expand on this even more: "Our job is to love others without stopping to inquire whether they are worthy or not." Of course, as easy as it is to agree with Gandhi and Merton, it is as difficult to live out their words. Loving and serving another is extremely demanding work, especially when that individual is unpleasantly different from us or we find that person offensive, or even the perpetrator of evil deeds. But we have that duty none-theless, even as we struggle to undo or reverse what that person may be doing in, or to, the community.

God reveals the God-self in mysterious ways. It is not about human logic, but about faith and our relationship in God and with others. As the old Christian saying goes, "Love the sinner, but hate the sin."

De León: Mevlana, what you are expressing is similar to the idea in *The Zohar* that God is manifest in the human community relative to the practice of virtue.

Rumi: Indeed, Rabbi! From my studies and from what I hear in our dialog, this impulse of virtuous and responsible living appears to be fairly common in the mysticism of most traditions, although we may explain it differently.

From my perspective, part of emptying ourselves to receive the Beloved is the giving of ourselves to others through altruism and works of justice, which we sometimes call, appropriately enough, self-sacrifice. In this sense, I have referred to myself as a "slave" in carrying out deeds of service with the joy of worship.

Thus it is that we must strive for a just society for all those whom the Beloved loves so that the Beloved can be in full union with us all. Justice flows from our relationship with the Beloved, and compels us to help provide marginalized people in the community with the security they need in their lives to have the opportunity to seek and receive the Beloved, which in turn, moves us all closer to being one, One.

Eckhart: Yes, I agree. We must be there for others in the labor of justice. Our new personal humanity that results from pushing aside the false ego must lead to service toward others, but not only in acts of charity, such as giving food to the poor, which is commendable and necessary; but we must also dedicate ourselves to changing social structures that cause poverty and require people to beg. Justice and mysticism go hand-in-hand.[7]

Justice is always an outcome of our relationship with God.[8] We thus sanctify our work, not vice versa.[9] For me, any act of justice, however small or humble, is nothing other than the birth of the Son of God that has occurred, and is always occurring.[10]

De León: Your last point resonates with me, Meister Eckhart. To reflect a difference between mysticism in the Abrahamic and Asian traditions, generally speaking, monotheistic and Western animist traditions tend to focus their mysticism on the Divine—a relationship with either a deity "out there" or a deity-consciousness within.

By contrast, in the Eastern religious traditions, as I understand it, the goal is to become one with, dissolved into, the One, and remain there; they focus on an impersonal absolute, uncovered in meditation. As Brother Teasdale will write in the 20th century: "To a person in the Hindu Vedantic tradition who follows the teaching of *advaita*—the primal unity or non-duality of all being—we are all already divine, and we simply have to wake up and realize it. And for Buddhists, the goal is the transpersonal awakening to boundless awareness, non-dual experience, and infinite compassion."[11]

Eckhart: Your mention of Brother Teasdale, Rabbi, fits right in with our discussion. He will integrate teachings from the world's religions with his own Catholic training, and combine his vigorous spiritual practice with the necessities of making a living and pursuing a course of social justice in a big American city.

De León: Yes, Brother Teasdale will be well-grounded in the spiritual traditions of the East, which he will come to realize do not advocate a life solely dedicated to meditation. Buddhists, for example, have a solid social justice tradition. I think sometimes it may be more of a question of spiritual emphasis.

Rumi: You are right, Rabbi, the story of the Buddha's enlightenment is a case in point. Siddhartha—who later became the Buddha—was born a prince and lived in great privilege. Because his father sensed something unusual about him and feared he might become a saint, instead of a ruler, he never allowed him to leave the palace.

After much coaxing, Siddhartha finally received permission to see first-hand the kingdom he would someday inherit. Initially, he only noticed how happy his citizens looked as they showered him with praise. But in this first city, he noticed an old, bent-over man, and understood that his father had tried to shelter him from the reality of aging; and this discovery disturbed him.

In the next city, people greeted him much the same way, but he encountered a person, who was sick, coughing, and pale. Siddhartha realized he also had been shielded from seeing people ill, and this greatly troubled him. The exuberant greeting in the third, final city was much like the first two; but this time he saw a funeral procession where mourners carried a dead person wrapped in white.

When Siddhartha returned to the palace, he reflected upon the reality that people get old and bent, that illness is a part of every life, and that every life ends in death. He became depressed and a recluse. What was he to make of all this?

One day, Siddhartha rode out on his chariot again, but this time to the countryside. It was here that his moment of mystical union occurred. He encountered a man, sitting under a tree, who had seen suffering in the world, but had decided to dedicate his life in meditation as a way to flee suffering through enlightenment.

The experience changed something in Siddhartha, and he decided at that moment that he would answer a call to search for truth and enlightenment in his own life. After a period of time and failed extreme asceticism, he did achieve enlightenment and became the Buddha. He realized complete insight into the cause of suffering, and the steps necessary to eliminate it. This liberation or peace of mind is to be free from ignorance, greed, hatred, and other afflictive states.

After this, the Buddha spent the last 45 years of his life, traveling the countryside, teaching enlightenment to all kinds of people, of every social strata, that suffering can be ended by the Noble Eightfold Path: right view, right intention, right speech, right action, right livelihood, right effort, right mindfulness, and right concentration; The Path has three main sections: wisdom, ethical conduct, and mental discipline.

What is interesting about the Buddha's story is that he did not hear a voice, or was not blinded for three days, or was not struck in a trance. Something as simple as meeting that man was life-changing and transformed his life and the course of history forever. Although a series of preceding actions created the opportunity for this decisive encounter, it was completely unsolicited and received passively by Siddhartha. Enlightenment was a force beyond his own that had seized him in its grasp, which, in turn, caused him to share it with others and be in self-less solidarity with their struggles. [12]

Indeed, people of the 20th and 21st centuries will have the good fortune of becoming familiar with Vietnamese monk Thich Nhat Hanh, a mystic, scholar, and peace activist. He will become one of the most beloved and influential Buddhist teachers in the West. He will be a war resister, and exiled from his country. He will speak eloquently about being "passionately present in the here and now" and that, "without a community, we cannot get very far." [13] Martin Luther King, Jr. will befriend him and nominate him for the Nobel Peace Prize.

De León: This is a perceptive insight into Buddhism. Thich Nhat Hanh is an excellent model. Thank you so much, Mevlana.

And speaking of Dr. King, Rabbi Heschel, whom I mentioned a bit ago, also will become a soul-mate of his. For both of them, their spirituality was intertwined intimately with political activism. After Rabbi Heschel joins Dr. King in the long 1965 march from Selma to Montgomery, Alabama, for voting rights, he will write of its spiritual significance for him: "For many of us the march . . . was about protest and prayer. Legs are not lips and walking is not kneeling. And yet our legs uttered songs. Even without words, our march was worship. I felt my legs were praying."[14]

As I observed earlier, in my Abrahamic tradition, one seeks to be united with the Godhead, but then return to help the world community. For us, according to *The Zohar*, justice is carrying out the *mitzvah*,[15] an act of justice, benevolence, or commandment, however humble, and is nothing less than part of what we call *Tikkun Olam*, which means "repairing the world" or "healing the world," mending the relationship between the world and God, and actually healing God. *Tikkun Olam* is our shared responsibility of making our human community better.

Rumi: A wonderful phrase and concept, Rabbi Moses! I truly appreciate your remarks, reflecting the responsibility of which you speak. In my own Sufi tradition, there will emerge a worldwide *hizmet* ("service") movement in the late 20th century, under the spiritual guidance of Fethullah Gülen.[16]

All in all, though, I look at it somewhat differently, more in interpretation than in result. As I see it, like all lovers, who strive to convey their love with something material, such as flowers, gifts, and so on, the Beloved created the world and continues to express the Divine's love through creation. We, in turn, show our love for God by how we love the holy creation and love others whom God has created since the beginning of time. As the 19th-century American mystic and naturalist Henry David Thoreau one day will write in his classic *Walden*, "Heaven is under our feet as well as over our heads."[17]

De León: Yes, Mevlana, quite true. For me, everything is linked with everything else. So, divine essence is below, as well as above, in heaven and on earth. There is nothing else.

Matthew Fox, centuries after us, writes that "Creation is what the mystic is awakened to and what the prophet fights to sustain"[18] —all creation, not just humanity. This unity with creation reminds me of Native American mystics, like Black Elk, who will say, "The first peace, which is the most important, is that which comes within the souls of people, when they realize their relationship, their oneness with the universe and all its powers and when they realize that, at the center of universe, dwells the Great Sprit and that this center is really everywhere; it is within each of us."[19]

Black Elk: Good evening, kind Sirs. I am not sure where I am. This type of place is strange and different from my home on the American Plains. I was sitting in a sweat lodge just now, contemplating *Wakan Tanka*, the Great Spirit, the Great Mystery, when I suddenly heard my name in the distance and now find myself sitting here with you wholly unexpectedly. This seems like a dream to me, but then sometimes dreams are wiser than waking.

Eckhart: Ah! We are pleased to have you with us, Black Elk. We recognize you as a *Wichasha Wakan*, or Spirit person of the Oglala Lakota people. We were just discussing the unity of all creation with the Divine, to whom you refer, it seems, as *Wakan Tanka*. Perhaps you might have some insight you would be generous enough to share with us?

Black Elk: I would be happy to recount for you a kind of ineffable mystical experience that happened when I was nine years old, just a child; but it impacted my whole life from then on out.

I suddenly had become extremely sick and was comatose for several days. During my illness, I had a vision in which the Thunder Beings (*Wakinyan*) visited me and took me in a flaming rainbow tipi to the Grandfathers, spiritual representatives of the six sacred directions (west, east, north, south, above, and below). I saw these spirits as kind and loving, full of years and wisdom, like revered human grandfathers.

In my vision, I was standing on the highest mountain of them all, and round about beneath me was the whole hoop of the world. And, while I stood there, I saw more than I can tell and I understood more than I saw, for I was seeing, in a sacred manner, the shapes of all things in the spirit, and the shape of all shapes as they must live together like one being. And I saw that the sacred hoop of my people was one of many hoops that made one circle, wide as daylight and as starlight, and in the center grew one mighty flowering tree to shelter all the children of one mother and one father. And I saw that it was holy.

Five years later, I tried to recount this vision to Black Road, a Sioux medicine man. However, I could never explain adequately the meaning of this mystical encounter, although I gleaned from it the wisdom to bring hope and healing to my people, to help flower the tree and keep it flowered, which I tried to do throughout my life. As I grew older, the meanings came clearer and clearer out of the pictures and the words; and, even now, I know that more was shown to me than I can tell.[20]

De León: This is an intense vision, Black Elk—a sacred hoop over which is the beautiful protective tree that we each should nourish and help bloom more and more. For me, this is a description of the Divine and our work to let the Divine flourish in all creation and among all peoples. I note interesting similarities with the Kabbalah, especially with the feminine side of God and the feminine Mother Earth of your tradition. Your description of the tree also reminds me of the whirling tree of God we speak of in the Kabbalah.

Black Elk: Thank you, Rabbi. I was happy to be called here to share my thoughts. However, I hear drums beating louder and louder in the distance, summoning me to council; and I must excuse myself. It was a pleasure. May *Wakan Tanka* be with you and upon you.

Eckhart: And peace be with you, Black Elk. Thank you for your insight, and thanks to *Wakan Tanka* for your presence among us. We shall meet again, I am sure.

Rumi: Wow, Black Elk was extraordinary! We were blessed to have him here.

His discussion of helping to flower the tree certainly reinforced my view that we need to measure the authenticity of spiritual experience by the extent to which it leads each of us to love and service. The less self-centered we become and the more self-less we are, the more we expand our labors on behalf of others. We become the light, and the shining of the light is the essence of our life in the world. A candle loses none of its light by lighting another. To the contrary, it makes the world brighter.

Eckhart: Very interesting, Mevlana. And similar to what Jesus said: "You are the light of the world." You have given me a deeper meaning for that wisdom saying of his.

Rumi: You know, Friends, it strikes me, as I listen to you, that mysticism, especially of our apophatic kind, can have a strong counter-cultural aspect and, in some respects, even resistance to social constructs, especially in politics and organized religion. Indeed, I detect a strong oppositional undercurrent, over the last few centuries, as mystical practice manifests itself in doing the Divine One's work here on earth. I think the Beguine and Beghard movements would be perfect examples, which is why the official church is often in conflict with them and tends to regard them as subversives.

Eckhart: Yes, excellent insight, Mevlana. In fact, the future seems to hold a parallel with the development of African American mysticism in the southern United States that began during the epoch of slavery and continued after its abolishment.[21]

Is there a bridge between mysticism and marginalization, I wonder? In other words, what is the extent to which oppression creates a mystical response—a response of seeking a deeper relationship with God outside religious structures that actually oppress people or provide support for such suppression? And a related question for me is to what extent does mysticism have, or should have, a revolutionary impact in society and its structures?

De León: I would remark that, in the Jewish tradition, we understand mystical exploration more as a community enterprise and sometimes as a defensive way of facing our own oppression by majority society.

Eckhart: Interesting, Rabbi. It seems to me these questions merit extensive exploration, though perchance at a later date. In the meanwhile, perhaps our readers will keep them in mind as they take what they may glean from our discussions into an examination of their own spiritual lives, especially as they might pertain to "birthing" a more just society. That is my hope.

De León: As it is mine, Meister Eckhart.

Rumi: Indeed.

De León: This has me thinking, dear Brothers. The mysticism of my tradition relies heavily on, and is typically limited to, the Kabbalah texts, which can have the effect of making it less intuitive and spontaneous than other traditions of mysticism practice. This may be part of the reason there seem to be fewer mystics, who stand out distinctly and individually, as Christian and Muslim mystics seem to do.

We do have some outstanding mystics, though. One I would greatly recommend for future generations is Martin Buber, and his classic *I and Thou*. Buber talks of God immanently present in the "I-Thou" encounter between two people. "Thou" refers to an intimacy with the other person, rather than the "you" of common everyday associations, with people with whom we have no intimate relationship. But that "I-Thou" relationship moves into an "I-We" relationship, encompassing the "Thou" of all people, a sense of intimacy with all people, as distinguished from the day-to-day mundaneness of existence in the world.

It strikes me that, no matter how we approach mysticism from within our own traditions, we do get to a common point, that mysticism involves intimacy with the community as much as it involves intimacy with the Divine—authentic mysticism should manifest itself in social activism—and that divine intimacy melds us into one, One.

Eckhart: Yes, good point, Rabbi. From my perspective, we will know that the Divine Word has been born in us partly by the way we behave and live our lives. The more and more clearly God's image shows in us, the more God is born in us.

Even though this birthing results in our own transformation, this union is not simply our new life in God, but also God's life in and through us, for this is the fullness of time, when the Son of God is begotten in us.[22] And God's birthing in us manifests itself in how we live in the human community.

Rumi: Yes, I absolutely concur. No matter how ecstatic and deep one's mystical experience, we cannot live in a vacuum, isolated from our communities. The Beloved wants to bring us all into union, not just the Beloved and me, but us all.

Eckhart: I am in wholehearted accord with your sentiments, Mevlana; and I think, with that summary statement, this may be a good juncture to move on to our next topic of the evening. I would wrap up this session of our dialogs, Friends, with two observations, the first of which is somewhat tangential to our conversation.

It is evident that all three of our Abrahamic mystical traditions have a deep sense of physicality, but Christian mysticism may be more "incarnational" than other traditions. We believe in God becoming human or incarnate in Jesus, becoming God's Son. We also observe the stigmata in mystics like the Apostle Paul, Francis of Assisi, and Catherine of Siena. The stigmata are sores or sensations of pain in locations corresponding to the crucifixion wounds of Jesus. This seems to happen more frequently with Christian women mystics.

Interestingly enough, this is also something we occasionally observe in Buddhist art. But we should reserve discussion on art and its multi-faceted relationships with religion and mysticism, a stimulating topic, until the next time we get together.

Secondly, and more to the point, I would note we have so much to learn from each other, if we are only open to listening to each other. And we would all be spiritually and personally richer for listening to one another. As you once wrote, Mevlana: "Not the ones speaking the same language, but the ones sharing the same feeling, understand each other."

NOTES

1. Shakespeare, *Macbeth* (Act 5, Scene 5, lines 27–28).
2. Besides Thomas Merton (1915–1968), one might identify Dorothy Day (1897–1980), Abraham Joshua Heschel (1907–1972), and Howard Thurman (1899–1981) as among the most significant social justice mystics and advocates in contemporary United States.
3. See Teresa of Ávila, *Interior Castle*, trans. E. Allison Peers (Mineola, NY: Dover Publications, 2007).
4. See Susan Rakoczy, *Great Mystics and Social Justice: Walking on the Two Feet of Love* (Mahwah, NJ: Paulist Press, 2006).
5. GaiamLife, "Stream of Consciousness," http://blog.gaiam.com/quotes/authors/gandhi?page=7; Ashoka, Forbes, "12 Great Quotes from Gandhi on His Birthday," Oct. 2, 2012, http://www.forbes.com/sites/ashoka/2012/10/02/12-great-quotes-from-gandhi-on-his-birthday.
6. See Rami Shapiro, *The Angelic Way: Angels through the Ages and Their Meaning for Us* (Katonah, NY: BlueBridge Books, 2009).
7. See Susan Rakoczy, *Scriptura*, 2013, "What Does Mysticism Have To Do With Social Justice?" http://scriptura.journals.ac.za/pub/article/view/84.
8. See, e.g., Dorothee Soelle, *The Silent Cry: Mysticism and Resistance*, trans. Barbara Rumscheidt and Martin Rumscheidt (Minneapolis: Fortress Press, 2001).
9. Meister Eckhart, "Do not think that saintliness comes from occupation; it depends rather on what one is. The kind of work we do does not make us holy, but we may make it holy."
10. Michael A. Sells, *Mystical Languages of Unsaying* (Chicago: University of Chicago, 1994), 7.
11. Wayne Teasdale, *The Mystic Heart: Discovering a Universal Spirituality in the World's Religions* (Novato, CA: New World Library, 2001), 25.
12. See Sungtaek Cho, *Urban Dharma*, "Selflessness: Toward a Buddhist Vision of Social Justice," http://www.urbandharma.org/udharma/towardjustice.html; and *Journal of Buddhist Ethics*, *Globethics*, http://www.globethics.net/web/journal-of-buddhist-ethics/journal-overview?layoutPlid=4297669.
13. Peace is the Way, May 12, 2013, "Oprah Winfrey talks with Thich Nhat Hanh Excerpt - Powerful," https://www.youtube.com/watch?v=NJ9UtuWfs3U.
14. Susannah Heschel, "Following in my father's footsteps: Selma 40 years later," *Vox of Dartmouth*, April 4, 2005, http://www.dartmouth.edu/~vox/0405/0404/heschel.html.
15. *Mitzvah* is Hebrew and refers to one of the 613 precepts and commandments given by God in the Torah at Mount Sinai, which is the source of all moral laws. It often has the connotation of a moral deed performed as a religious duty or an act of human kindness.
16. See Fethullah Gülen, http://fgulen.com/en (English version, and available in 31 other languages); Muhammed Çetin, *The Gülen Movement: Civic Service without Borders*. New York: Blue Dome Press, 2009.

17. Henry David Thoreau, *Walden* (Boston: Houghton Mifflin and Company, 1906), 313.

18. Matthew Fox, *Creation Spirituality: Liberating Gifts for the Peoples of the Earth* (New York: HarperOne, 1991), 10.

19. Wayne Teasdale, *The Mystic Hours: A Daybook of Inspirational Wisdom and Devotion* (Novato, CA: New World Library, 2004), 14.

20. Raymond J. DeMallie, "The Sixth Grandfather: Black Elk's Teachings Given to John G. Neihardt" (Lincoln, NE: University of Nebraska Press, 1984), 6–7.

21. See Erika DeSimone and Fidel Louis, *Voices Beyond Bondage: An Anthology of Verse by African Americans of the 19th Century* (Montgomery, Al; NewSouth Books, 2014).

22. Matthew Fox, *Meditations with Meister Eckhart* (Rochester, VT: Bear & Company, 1983), 84.

Chapter Eleven

Women and the Feminine

Ironic, but one of the most intimate acts of our body is death.
So beautiful appeared my death—knowing who then I would kiss,
I died a thousand times before I died.
"Die before you die," said the Prophet Muhammad.
Have wings that feared ever touched the Sun?
I was born when all I once feared—I could love.

—Rabi'a al-Adawiya

Rumi: Well, dear Brothers, if you do not mind, I will kick off this session. When I was preparing for this meeting and looking over some of the mysticism literature of the past and of the years to come, I was much surprised, and pleasantly so, by so many Christian women mystics. They have played an enormous role, though often unacknowledged for such, in developing mystical thought and ideas.

We do not observe this phenomenon as much in Islam, although we do have some well-respected woman mystics. One bright star in the mystical heavens is Rabi'a al-Adawiya, who lived in 8th-century Basra and helped reorient Muslim ascetics from a culture of awe and fear of Allah toward one of reaching intimacy with Allah through Allah's love.

Rabi'a al-Adawiya: Hello, Mevlana, and Rabbi Moses, and Meister Eckhart. Good evening. I am not at all sure how I ended up here. I was preparing myself for another date with the Beloved, when I heard my name whispered from deep within; and now suddenly I find myself sitting at this table with you at such a late hour.

De León: What a godsend, Rabi'a, that you are here; your radiance is even more striking than how your peers described you while you were here on earth.

Rabi'a al-Adawiya: Thank you, Rabbi, for the generous words. But whatever radiance there is, it is of my Beloved in whom I live.

Rumi: I was just mentioning to my colleagues your impact on mysticism in our tradition, especially with Sufis, and reorienting us toward love and intimacy with God, instead of living in dread and awe of God. You also were most adamant in getting the message out that mysticism was for everyone and not just for a select few.

Rabi'a al-Adawiya: Yes, Mevlana, it was always my goal, actually the goal of the Beloved through me, to help make mystical experience more accessible to middle and lower socioeconomic people, without the need for clerical intermediaries. The Beloved does not restrict mystical union to the elite or clerical classes, but wants to be in love with everybody and have everyone in love with the Beloved. My message fits squarely with a theme about which I am sure you have conversed this evening: mysticism is for all people, for every person who opens her or his heart to the Divine.

And, yes, it was imperative to shift people from relating to God in awe and fear, as a terrible person outside of ourselves, into experiencing a relationship with God as the Beloved, the Lover. One cannot be in love with a terrible and fearful "other." That "other" blocks the Beloved from our hearts. In fact, I composed a poem about this:

> O God, if I worship you for fear of Hell, burn me in Hell,
> and if I worship you in hope of Paradise,
> exclude me from Paradise.
> But if I worship you for Your Own sake,
> grudge me not your everlasting Beauty. [1]

Rumi: Concise and to the point, Rabi'a; and it recalls to mind another of your poignant poems:

> I have loved You with two loves—
> a selfish love and a love worthy of You.
> As for the love which is selfish,
> therein I occupy myself with You,
> to the exclusion of all others.
> But in the love which is worthy of You,
> You raise the veil that I may see You.
> Yet the praise is not mine in this or that,
> but the praise is to You in both that and this. [2]

Rabi'a al-Adawiya: Thank you, Mevlana, for reciting this in such a passionate way. I have always felt my personal history and background helped make me a better unworthy vessel for the Beloved and gave me enormous empathy for the people I sought to serve.

My family was extremely poor. In fact, my parents perished in a famine. I had the traumatic misfortune of being separated from my dear sisters and became homeless and destitute. A man seized me on the street and sold me into slavery for a pittance; but another man came to take pity on me, gained possession of me, and eventually gave me my freedom.[3]

Somehow, through the Beloved working in me, I became able to heal people and bless them with the Beloved's love. Despite being offered money, houses, and marriage proposals, I preferred to remain single and live in humble surroundings—in "the desert of God," as we say, but in the glorious love of the Divine. I lived to be 80 years old, something quite unusual in those days, and died in Jerusalem.

For me, oneness with God, and God alone, was the only existence I could fathom. In this oneness, I encountered my true self, a self I could not distinguish from my relationship with the Beloved: "For me, there is none, for I have ceased to exist, having passed out of self. I exist in God and am all together God's."[4] I am sure this is a topic you Gentlemen will discuss from a variety of perspectives this evening.

However, as much as I would like to engage in further conversation with you, I feel I am slipping away from you. It must be time to keep my date with the Beloved and take my leave from you, which I respectfully do. I kiss the hands of each of you and of the Divine in you. I regret I could not spend more time here with you. May our paths cross again, and soon. Good evening, kind Gentleman.

Eckhart: Take care, dear Rabi'a. We bless you and thank you for sharing so ardently the Divine in you.

Rumi: What a fortunate visit from Rabi'a. She became renowned as a saint, a woman who lost herself in union with the Divine. We Sufis sometimes refer to her as the "second spotless Mary." We revere Rabi'a for her graceful use of strikingly romantic imagery in expressing her relationship with God.

Rabi'a did much to foster gender egalitarianism within Sufism, to such an extent that the great Sufi master Ibn al-'Arabi would later say that women should be able to lead prayers in a mosque with mixed female and male congregations, a rather startling proposition for his time.

There were even many women in the Sufi orders, who, following Rabi'a's example, lived without marrying, despite cultural pressure and the strong suggestion of the Qur'an and the *hadith* to marry. Rabi'a's expression of selfless *mahabba* (love) would become a dominant theme in Sufism over the next several centuries after her.[5]

De León: She is obviously a saint, Mevlana, and a path blazer.

In Rabi'a's discussion of getting rid of her "self," I recalled a similarity within mystical Judaism. As our friend Professor Soltes will note about the fullest experience of mystical union, "Kabbalah expresses the profound yearning for direct human communion with God achieved through the anni-hilation of the individual's own personality—*Bittul ha-Yesh* (literally, 'anni-hilation or cancellation of the what-there-is [of myself]).' In this latter sense, we recognize the danger to all but the few who can manage self-annihilation and mergence into the One that yet leads to a return to the self and also have the ability to improve the condition of their community *(profanus)* based on the experience of *Bittul ha-Yesh.*"[6]

As the ego-self encounters the fullness of the *Eyn Sof* ("Infinite" or "End-less One"), the ego-self is dissolved, even though the individual remains a part of the Eyn Sof. This new self does not emerge through shame or dimin-ishment, as with ascetic mystical groups that practice mortification of flesh. Nor is the new self so caught up in blissful union that the individual ceases to function in society. Instead, the old self is transformed into a being so wrapped up in identity with God that ego, with all is trappings and con-structs, is annihilated.

Nevertheless, I am afraid that the patriarchal structure of all three of our social cultures and religious traditions has been less than conducive to wom-en spiritual leaders, and undoubtedly detrimental to them. But, despite this sinful oppression, I notice a large number of women mystics in the Christian tradition. I wonder, Meister Eckhart, how you would account for that?

Eckhart: Yes, Rabbi Moses, this is an interesting and astute observation. Indeed, women mystics in my area of the Holy Roman Empire, including some in the Beguine movement, have helped fashion part of my own think-ing.[7] As we know, the Beguines, a women's association, at times is at odds with the mainline religious establishment, as are the Beghards, a comparable men's organization.

The Beguine women live together in community and practice the Gospel, humbly serving the poor and following a lifestyle of poverty. Their Gospel witness sharply contrasts with, and challenges, those holding the reins of church power amid luxury. There are extraordinary women leaders among the Beguines, something that especially seems to alarm the authorities, who view them as subversive. But, then again, I must say, neither do the Beghard men avoid officialdom's wrath.

Marguerite Porete, the respected Beguine mystic, is a tragic case in point. In fact, I went to teach in Paris a year after the Inquisitor William of Paris had her executed and burned her book *The Mirror of Simple Souls* as heret-ical. William was a fellow Dominican friar; and we resided in the same community house in Paris. This was a very uncomfortable living situation, obviously; but I got to know much about Marguerite as a result because I attained access to some of William's files and listened to some of his discus-sions, albeit biased against her. Of course, others with whom I spoke were much more sympathetic. It was clear she had a following among the faithful, which was disconcerting to the clerical leaders, to say the least.

Marguerite Porete: Greetings, honorable Gentlemen. I am sorry to appear here so suddenly before you and perhaps startle you. I was actually preparing for a trip here to Venice, when, from what seemed far off, I heard my name invoked as a gentle invitation, summoning me, and then suddenly here I am.

Eckhart: Welcome, my dear Marguerite. I was just sadly recounting your tragic demise at the hands of the Inquisition. Your teachings triggered such fear in the theologians and authorities. Your untimely tragic death was an immense loss for us all.

Marguerite Porete: Whether it was a loss is not mine to say. God works mysteriously within us. I am completely in God's hands, enveloped by God's love, and hopefully one with God.

What intensely troubled the authorities was my teaching that our own deeds of virtue do not bring us into union with God. Instead, that union, with its definitive surrender and loss of self, causes us to exhibit the virtuous labor of God in our lives. That, of course, was quite different from what my opponents believed; their idea was that our own good deeds brought about union with God. Frankly, I believe steadfastly that my view was right and came from my union with God. It is our surrender to God that lets God operate in us.

Even though my views ended up with the same practical effect of a virtuous life being lived, this happened, or could happen, without intermediary ecclesial hierarchs. God did it on God's own. My opponents simply could not deal with this "heresy" or thinking "outside the box" of their belief structure and patriarchal hegemony.

Indeed, William and others were fiercely hell-bent on removing me from society. He degraded me as a *pseudo-mulier* ("fake-woman"), "pseudo" because I lived outside of, and often in opposition to, the religious and cultural stereotypes imposed on us women. Nor could they handle my revolutionary use of sexuality and gender equality in referring to God. My spirituality turned the negativity associated with women and gender roles on their head, as did my gender dynamic about the three *personas* of God, the Trinity. It was a little too unique for their stultified way of thinking. They accused me of usurping the male-reserved function of leading people into union with the sacred.

I wrote that, in mystical union, the church was unnecessary, as indeed was everything else. All one need do was take on nothingness to become ecstatically united by, and with, the Divine Lover. Rather than trying to understand what I meant and the kind of apophatic, unsaying language I was using, they burned me at the stake as a heretic and as many copies of my book they could get their hands on.

They even took umbrage that I wrote in vernacular French, and not official Latin—of course, fearing it would "corrupt" the minds of ordinary folk. I steadfastly refused to recant, withdraw my book from circulation, or even speak to the Inquisition. I could not do otherwise without betraying God. Death for me was but another step into the arms of the Divine Lover.

Eckhart: My dear Sister, you were so courageous, resolute, and calm to the end. It was quite astounding how the crowd reacted to your fiery death at the stake. They saw you die as a holy woman and martyr, and wept and murmured that it was wrong to have killed you. I thank you on behalf of all of the thousands of us who have become closer, and will become closer, to God because of your hallowed work and righteous example.

Marguerite Porete: Thank you for your gentle and generous words, Meister Eckhart; but they belong as praise to God, not to me.

I think I must leave now. The gondola has arrived to taxi me over to the convent where Mechthild of Hackeborn is staying. Hildegard of Bingen and Rabi'a al-'Adawiya will be joining us in the early morning. I am sure our companionship together this evening is only one of many such occasions down the road.

Rumi: Thank you so much, Marguerite, for gracing us with your presence this evening. You remind me so much of Rabi'a al-'Adawiya, our celebrated and fearless Sufi mystic teacher. Peace be upon you.

Marguerite Porete: Ah, I am honored and humbled by the comparison. Blessings upon you, Mevlana, and upon you Rabbi Moses and Meister Eckhart. We shall meet again soon, I am sure. We all live in the same home. Take care.

De León: What a fortuitous appearance of Marguerite among us!

Eckhart: As you know, Marguerite's revolutionary beliefs and writings became known as a mysticism of Divine Love, presented in ecstatic, and sometimes erotic and sexual, fashion. Mystics like Marguerite will even speak of being ravished by God. Catherine of Siena and Teresa of Ávila,[8] who follow after her, and probably prompted by Catherine's example, likewise will articulate a sensual expression of mystical union with God.[9]

Both Catherine's and Teresa's passionate mysticism will find expression in art. Early next century, Giovanni di Paolo will unveil his famous painting of Catherine's "Mystical Marriage" with Jesus; and, in the mid-1600s, Gian Lorenzo Bernini will carve a magnificent rapturous sculpture of the "Ecstasy of Saint Teresa," based on her autobiography's narrative of an encounter with an angel:

> I saw in his hand a long spear of gold; and, at the iron's point, there seemed to be a little fire. He appeared to me to be thrusting it at times into my heart, and to pierce my very entrails; when he drew it out, he seemed to draw them out also, and to leave me all on fire with a great love of God. The pain was so great, that it made me moan; and yet so surpassing was the sweetness of this excessive pain, that I could not wish to be rid of it. The soul is satisfied now with nothing less than God. The pain is not bodily, but spiritual; though the body has its share in it. It is a caressing of love so sweet which now takes place

between the soul and God, that I pray God of His goodness to make the person experience it who may think that I am lying. [10]

De León: Astounding, and sensual indeed, but descriptive of Teresa's mystical writings. It is quite captivating. I am proud to note as a historical side bar that Ávila, where I finally settled, for its relatively small population, was home to so many mystics and spiritual writers of all three of our traditions.

But back to the topic at hand. When I listen to you, Meister Eckhart, and to Marguerite Porete and the others talk about the oppression of women mystics, I get a chill up my spine. On the one hand, I admire how both you and Ms. Porete engage in an apophatic treatment of gender with respect to God, just as I was trying to do in *The Zohar*. [11] It is engrossing that the three of us make this shift away from God as only masculine at about the same time in history.

But I also agonize about the extent to which the astonishing mysticism of these inspiring holy women might also be a response to the oppression of women in society during these times, similar, as we mentioned earlier, with other systems of suppression.

Eckhart: They killed Marguerite, but they could not kill her spirit or her book. *The Mirror of Simple Souls*, written as a play in 122 chapters, will remain enormously popular in vernacular languages throughout the medieval era, but will lose the identity of its authorship. Ironically, it will be published in the early 20th century with official church approval, but without her name attached to it. It will not be clear at the time who the author is until 1946. She will remain an outstanding figure of mysticism, and *The Mirror* will take its rightful place as an exceptional classic of Christian love mysticism. Her death vindicated her as much as her life did.

With respect to your earlier question, Rabbi Moses, about the rise of individual Christian mystics. Certainly, the Beguine movement had something to do with the number of women Christian mystics, but perhaps another salient reason is the institution of convents, which offer women opportunities to live in community, usually as monastic nuns, for study, reflection, and contemplation.

At times, there would be no other alternative by which some women could support themselves, given the greater numbers of women than men in society, owing, in part, to all the wars. For other women, their only other choice typically would be to marry, have children, and help eke out a scrabble of a living for their families.

Their celibate lifestyle received exalted and protected status in the church (as Brides of Christ). Likewise, the cult of the Virgin Mary helped garner respect for the role of women, both for those who were mothers as well as for women who were celibate. Some women mystics literally attached themselves to churches as anchorites, where they lived in small huts, prayed, and offered spiritual advice to community folks or pilgrims.

This paradoxically allowed women to develop a more ecstatic, even erotic, description of the mystical experience since they were describing a love relationship with male personages of God or Jesus. Social convention keeps men from expressing such erotic love toward another man, although you, Mevlana, came the nearest in your poetry about your close friend and spiritual teacher Shams of Tabriz.

Rumi: Yes, the women mystics show us that mystical language is best as the language of the bedroom. In generations to come, alas, I fear people some will interpret my love poetry only as about human love, even erotic love. But they miss the point. My poetry is all about the love relationship with the Beloved and the intensity of that consummate union. The best I can do, of course, is write in human terms to express an all-consuming, passionate divine union, for which my words are but dim shadows.

There is an interesting flip-side to this, is there not, Rabbi Moses, with respect to your Bible and the Song of Songs, which we also know as the Song of Solomon? It is an astonishingly eloquent love song of erotic and sexual affection, nowhere mentioning Adonai (Yahweh), but clearly a beautiful work of poetry, much like Shakespeare.

De León: Yes, Mevlana, you are correct. Its eroticism and sexual passion made it controversial; and, for that reason, it was the last book admitted to the canon of the *Tanahk*, the Hebrew Bible. Most scholars in the future will come to believe that it was so exquisite that people just did not want to jettison it. Thus, individuals and groups made up stories about it, such as attributing authorship to Solomon, so as to justify inclusion in the Bible. The Jews then transformed it into an allegory of Adonai's bond with Israel; and Christians, of Christ with the church.

Rumi: But, you know, Rabbi, that is exactly how I think we can use such an erotic genre of poetry to express utter intimacy with the Lover. I do it all the time—as many mystics have done, and will do. Ironically, as I mentioned, people sometimes take my ecstatic poems about passionate union with the Lover as only romantic poems, pure and simple—sort of the Song of Songs technique in reverse.

De León: Well, in any regard, it is now one of the overtly mystical biblical texts for the Kabbalah; and, following the dissemination of *The Zohar*, Jewish mysticism took on a metaphorically anthropomorphic erotic element—the Song of Songs being an example of this.

Rabbi Rami Shapiro, in the 21st century, will re-translate the Song, restoring all its eroticism and interpreting it as a celebration of the love between the Divine Feminine and the contemporary spiritual seeker.[12]

Though I must say, Gentlemen, speaking of irony, insofar as Jewish mysticism, especially the Kabbalah, relates to interpretation of the Torah, no matter how erotically or sexually expressed, the interpretative and custodial role over Kabbalah was always kept within the purview of men in our community. That unfortunate exclusion was sometimes rationalized as women being "naturally" attuned to the Divine and thus not in "need" of the Kabbalah.

The Kabbalah's mystical tradition gives the Divinity a feminine side; we move toward understanding and experiencing the Divine not only as masculine, but also as feminine, even though we understand God as genderless. Indeed, we view the masculine side of God as the transcendent side, the male God who exiled Adam and Eve from the Garden. And, for us, the feminine side of God is the immanent side, the presence or tabernacle of God, *Shekhinah*.

Yet, paradoxically, as we discussed earlier, despite all the emphasis on the feminine side of God, women are not permitted to be part of Kabbalah practice. Nor do we see a "break out" of Jewish women mystics as in the Christian tradition. In fact, because the Kabbalah is a community mystical experience, we do not seem to have a "break out" of as many individual Jewish male mystics as there are these days in the Christian and Sufi traditions. Fortunately, that will begin to change in the 20th and 21st centuries.

Eckhart: Thanks for re-directing us a bit, Rabbi. You have touched on an enthralling aspect of reported mystical experience not much discussed in religious practice. Although 20th-century theologians will write and speak on deconstructing the patriarchal god model, what is different here is the sometimes-mystical experience and description of the Divine as feminine, which is much more frequent than people might think.

In 1963, Thomas Merton, the Christian mystic whom I mentioned earlier, will publish "Hagia Sophia" ("Holy Wisdom"), which depicts the feminine side of God as an emanation of "the glory" of God: "His light is diffused in the air and the light of God is diffused by Hagia Sophia . . . . The Diffuse shining of God is Hagia Sophia. We call her His 'glory.' In Sophia His power is experienced only as mercy and as love."[13] This parallels, Rabbi Moses, how the Kabbalah describes God's immanent, feminine side, *Shekhinah*. Rabbi Shapiro, whom we mentioned earlier, also will write of Sophia in the same insight.[14]

De León: Fascinating. Thank you for sketching that parallel, Meister Eckhart.

Rumi: You know, Gentlemen, Julian of Norwich, the English anchoress and remarkable Christian mystic, has always intrigued me. She will come a few decades after us, and use feminine images in her mystical writings, such as Jesus as a mother breastfeeding us, Jesus in labor on the cross, and Jesus as a hen with her chicks.[15] This certainly is refreshing imagery for spiritual writings that are overly dominated by male analogies and allegories.

She draws proper attention to what we might call the feminine side of God, a richness and fullness we would otherwise lose. Actually, Rabbi, when you were describing the masculine and feminine sides of God, a passage from Julian's *Revelations of Divine Love* came to mind: "As truly as God is our Father, so truly is God our Mother . . . to the property of Motherhood belong nature, love, wisdom, and knowledge and this is God."[16]

Eckhart: Thank you, Mevlana, for mentioning this insight of hers. The letters of Catherine of Siena and *The Cloud of Unknowing* apparently will deeply influence Julian. *The Cloud of Unknowing*, to be written later in this century, will take root as a masterpiece of Christian mysticism; and Catherine, although living for only thirty-three years, will emerge as a gifted theologian and mystic.

De León: I would remark that, for my tradition, a feminist theology will develop in the 20th and 21st centuries that not only challenges the historical discrimination against women in religious conventions, but will take issue with how we view God and with the power model and philosophy that underpin patriarchal structures. I know it will happen as well in Christian theology, while perhaps not much noticeably in Islam as of that juncture in history, although there will be a few stirrings in that regard, one being Aisha Abd al-Rahman.[17]

In the Jewish tradition, Judith Plaskow, a distinguished professor of religious studies, will author a masterwork, *Standing Again at Sinai*, which will pierce through ages-old struggles with patriarchy: its hegemony over the narrative of our Jewish history and religious texts, its privilege in defining the Jewish community and distributing power within it, and its self-justification for using masculine God-language.

Professor Plaskow will be the first Jewish feminist to identify herself as a theologian and advocate vigorously for use of feminist methodologies to uncover Jewish women's history and cultures and the need to use feminist *midrash* and liturgy to reshape Jewish memory, past and present. She will emphasize that the pluralism of the past must include the pluralism of women's experiences. In her view, law is a necessary element of all human cultures, but that it must be "a shared communal process."[18]

Susannah Heschel, Judith Plaskow, and Starhawk: Excuse us, learned Gentlemen. We are not sure how we ended up at this table next to yours. We were enjoying an *almuerzo* on the sunny *zócolo* in Mexico City. We are, or were, there for an international WomenSpirit Rising conference at the Colegio Sor Juana Inés de la Cruz, named after a 17th-century nun and the Americas' first feminist writer.[19]

Susannah Heschel: Yes, and the next thing we knew we are sitting here in this quaint medieval-looking tavern where everyone is in period dress. And we could not but overhear you mention Judith by name.

De León: Susannah! I recognize you. You are Rabbi Abraham Joshua Heschel's daughter, are you not? Permit me to introduce ourselves. This is Mevlana Jalal ad-Din Rumi and Meister Eckhart; and I am Moses de León. We are in period dress, as you call it, because this is what we wear. This is Venice at the turn of the 14th century.

Judith Plaskow: Amazing! How did we get here? For us, we are well into the 21st century. What a surprise and honor to meet the three of you. And this is our friend, Starhawk, who is also Jewish, but has moved away from Judaism, partly because of its patriarchal power configuration, among other reasons. She is a voice in current earth-based spirituality.

Eckhart: Starhawk?

Starhawk: Yes, pleased to meet you all, especially at the time of the Summer Solstice. I identify myself as a celebrator of the Goddess movement and Earth-based feminist spirituality. I am also a peace, environment, and global justice activist and trainer, and a Pagan and a witch. [20]

My spirituality is linked to my feminism, which is about challenging unequal power structures that lead to inequalities in race, class, sexual orientation, gender identity, and so on. We need not just change who holds power, but change how we conceive of power.

There is the power we are all familiar with—power *over*. But there is another kind of power—power from *within*. For a woman, it is the power to be fertile in terms of having babies, writing books, dancing, baking bread, or being a great community organizer. It is the kind of power that does not depend on depriving someone else. [21]

Rumi: Very well said, superbly astute, and a radical reorientation of concepts of power—not just challenging the subsidiary role to which religious traditions have historically relegated women. Hints of this power-shift idea, as well as describing the Divine in feminine terms, have come up with mystics we discussed earlier.

Plaskow: Religious language and symbols legitimate social systems. If the Ineffable God is portrayed as a dominating male, human institutions are likely to be male-dominated. Thus, the exploration of God-language is tied inextricably to justice and authority in human community. I would argue passionately for pluralistic imagery of divinity within monotheism so that the imagery translates into "the presence of God in empowered, egalitarian community." [22]

Eckhart: I certainly agree with you Professor Plaskow, and applaud your work to move us all in that direction.

Rumi: Ms. Heschel, I have some sort of prescient understanding that you are a preeminent professor on Jewish, Islamic, and Christian studies. It is wonderful to meet you. We have been discussing your father from time to time this evening, and have such great respect for him. Rabbi Moses, in fact, noted his "praying with legs" insight about his march with Dr. Martin Luther King from Selma to Montgomery.

Susannah Heschel: Thank you kindly, Mevlana, for the wonderful recollection of my father. My father's words about Dr. King should remind us that each Jew can be a prophetic voice, an echo of the prophets of Israel from whom we are descended. He would have wanted us to end the bitterness that often poisons our political debates and unite together in overcoming enmity, selfishness and injustice. Perhaps he would have enjoined us to finally accomplish what the prophets demand, and create the society that would make them proud.[23] Of course, what my father said would apply to all the Abrahamic traditions that accept the ancient prophets of Israel.

Plaskow: This is such an enchanting encounter. I regret that we cannot stay long. We are anxious to get outside and take our bearings to find our way back to Mexico City, where we were gathering for the conference that Susannah had convened.

But one last comment. With regard to the snippet of your conversation that we could not but help overhear, I assure you that times will change; and, by the 20th century, more and more women will rightfully take their places as spiritual scholars and leaders and often will apply a feminist perspective. We will not yet be where we need to be, but much further along the path than in your century.

Eckhart: This is heartening to know. And, dear Friends, before you take your leave to return Mexico City, you actually may be in the right place at the right time. Mechthild of Hackeborn, Hildegard of Bingen, Marguerite Porete, and Rabi'a al-Adawiya are all gathering in the morning at the Convento Lucis Divinae. Perhaps you might like to meet up with them since you all are kindred spirits.

Heschel: Wonderful news! Perhaps that is another reason for our being brought here. We would love to join them. I so love the coincidental mysteriousness of this all or maybe it is not so coincidental after all. And perhaps they can help us somehow return to Mexico City afterwards.

Eckhart: The tavern keeper is a kind man. I am sure he will escort you to a taxi gondola outside that will ferry you to the convent.

Starhawk: Thank you, and, with that, Gentlemen, we must be on our way. We cannot tarry, given the lateness of the hour. We bid you good evening. Blessed be. We have gained much insight from your learned conversation; and we hope our presence has helped expand your understanding, as well.

Rumi: Good evening, Friends. Merry meet, and merry part. I am sure we will have the pleasure of being with each other again as time goes on.

De León: What a blessing that was to get such a privileged glimpse into the future with such wonderful women. I must say it has been extraordinary, to say the least, and a gift that so many distinguished people from past and future have been calling at our table.

Rumi : I am happy we picked this topic of women and the feminine because it is such an impressive and powerful current of mysticism throughout the centuries, but one that has not received the attention and respect it deserves.

I am also pleased about this fortuitous visit. It was a fitting conclusion to this part of our dialog. I recall that the Buddha reasoned that males and females had an equal capacity for awakening. We are reminded tonight that women and men have an equal capacity for awakening spirituality and mysticism in each other.

NOTES

1. "Rabi'a al-Adawiya," *Sufimaster*, http://sufimaster.org/adawiyya.htm.

2. Ibid.

3. See Atticus Frost, April 30, 2013, "A Quick Lesson on Rabi'a of Sufism," https://www.youtube.com/watch?v=hysq3Eb3ADM; Joseph Barry Martin, Dec. 3, 2013, "Rabia-al-Adawiyya, Female Sufi Mystic," https://www.youtube.com/watch?v=xkUmGulELcc; Imam Haya's Channel, Aug. 16, 2009, "Rabia al Adawiyya—With My Beloved," https://www.youtube.com/watch?v=Wro84VilG8o; Sister Marie Keyrouz, Nov. 30, 2012, "Rabi'a al Adawiya," https://www.youtube.com/watch?v=poWfUVW8k3c. For a hagiographical account of Rabi'a's life, see "Rabi'a Basri," http://www.rumi.org.uk/sufism/rabia.htm.

4. See "Rabi'a al-Adawiyya or Rabi'a al-Qaysiyya," http://www.contemplativespirit uality.org/media/ifaith2010rabia.pdf.

5. Ori Z. Soltes, *Mysticism in Judaism, Christianity, and Islam: Searching for Oneness* (Lanham, MD: Rowman & Littlefield, 2009), 76.

6. Ibid., 105–06.

7. See Bernard McGinn, *Meister Eckhart and the Beguine Mystics: Hadewijch of Brabant, Mechthild of Magdeburg, and Marguerite Porete* (London: Bloomsbury Publishing, 1997); *and* see Glenn E. Myers, *Seeking Spiritual Intimacy: Journeying Deeper with Medieval Women of Faith* (Nottingham, England: Inter-Varsity Press. 2011); Emilie ZumBrunn, *Women Mystics in Medieval Europe* (St. Paul, MN: Paragon House, 1998).

8. Professor Soltes points out that Teresa of Ávila (1515–1582) had a *converso* background (Spanish Jews or Muslims who converted to Christianity under force) and a love affair, both of which narrowed her life options and propelled her toward the convent. In the century before Teresa, the Beguines had begun to affiliate with the Carmelites. Teresa joined the Carmelites in 1535, and ultimately became one the country's tireless reformers of religious communities. Her most famous disciple was the mystic John of the Cross (San Juan de la Cruz) (1542–1591), also from Ávila. Soltes, *Mysticism in Judaism, Christianity, and Islam*, 151–53. John was a fellow reformer of the church, the "father of Spanish poetry," and also had a *converso* background. Both Teresa and John were familiar with Kabbalah.

9. See Teresa of Avila, *The Life of Saint Teresa of Avila by Herself*, trans. J. M. Cohen (New York: Penguin Books, 1988) (Chapter XXIX, pt. 17).

10. Ibid., 226

11. For an enlightening treatment of this theme, see Michael A. Sells, *Mystical Languages of Unsaying* (Chicago: University of Chicago, 1994), 180–205 ("Porete and Eckhart: The Apophasis of Gender").

12. *Embracing the Divine Feminine: Finding God Through God the Ecstasy of Physical Love - The Song of Songs Annotated & Explained*, trans. Rami Shapiro (Woodstock, VT: SkyLight Paths Publishing, 2014).

13. "Merton—Hagia Sophia," Eternal Feminine, http://eternalfeminine.wikispaces.com/Merton+-+Hagia+Sophia.

14. Rami Shapiro, *The Divine Feminine in Biblical Wisdom: Selections Annotated & Explained* (Woodstock, VT: SkyLight Paths Publishing, 2005).

15. Julian of Norwich, *Revelations of Divine Love* (Short Text and Long Text), trans. Elizabeth Spearing (New York: Penguin Books, 2003). This is the oldest surviving book in the English language by a woman author.

16. See "Revelations of Divine Love by Julian of Norwich," Sept. 4, 2013, https://www.youtube.com/watch?v=3z0er8lToUQ (full audiobook).

17. Aisha Abd al-Rahman (1913–1998), Egyptian author who published under the name Bint al-Shati ("Daughter of the Riverbank"), was the second modern woman to undertake Qur'anic exegesis.

18. Judith Plaskow, *Standing Again at Sinai: Judaism from a Feminist Perspective* (New York: HarperOne, 1991), 71.

19. "Sor Juana Inés de la Cruz: Biography," *Bio*, http://www.biography.com/people/sor-juana-in%C3%A9s-de-la-cruz-38178#synopsis.

20. "Starhawk's Tangled Web," http://www.starhawk.org/.

21. Carol Christ and Judith Plaskow (eds.), *Womanspirit Rising: A Feminist Reader in Religion* (New York: Harper & Row, 1979), 259 (Starhawk, "Witchcraft and Women's Culture").

22. Plaskow, *Standing Again at Sinai*, 155.

23. Susannah Heschel, "Their Feet Were Praying: Remembering the inspiration Heschel and King drew from each other," *The Jewish Week*, Jan. 10, 2012, http://www.thejewishweek.com/editorial_opinion/opinion/their_feet_were_praying.

Chapter Twelve

As Dawn Approaches

Mysticism and the 21st Century

You have no idea how hard I have looked
for a gift to bring you.
Nothing seemed right.
What is the point of bringing gold to
the gold mine, or water to the sea.
Everything I came up with was like
taking spices to the Orient.
It is no good giving my heart and my
soul because you already have these.
So I have brought you a mirror.
Look at yourself and remember me. [1]

—Rumi

De León: Well, it is long past midnight; and the fog has begun to roll in. I expect dawn will be upon us by the time we finish our discussion and our last pot of yet another exotic tea from the Orient. I think we should have one more taste of the tavern's hand-made pistachio gelato. We have nothing like this in my part of the world. It is so creamy and delicious.

Mevlana, you are on the way to being one of the most read poets in the world and a huge hit in what will become the United States and Canada. That is solid respect for what you tap into with your impassioned poetry, which is often pithy but always powerful. Perhaps you have some insights about mysticism you would like to impart to our 21st-century readers?

Rumi: Thank you, Rabbi Moses. You are unduly kind.

I think I am struck most about the similarities in our understanding and expressions of mystical union. Even though we come out of different religious traditions with diverse doctrinal teachings, albeit all three of Abrahamic origin, it looks as if we have common steps to mystical union, even though we describe the steps, and how they happen, differently. First is surrendering, emptying one's self. Next is being filled with and powerfully united with divine and sacred love. Third is acting with good or justice toward everyone in the human community and life itself. These are not necessarily successive steps, but can overlap or occur simultaneously.

De León: I respectfully concur, Mevlana, and would add only that this journey is a long one; it takes much effort and time, a few years, with constant dedication and rigorous personal discipline, or perhaps the course of one's entire life. What is certain is that one's journey is always ongoing. But, once one discovers that she or he is on the path, that individual will find joy in the arduous journey, even if the trek takes us through the "dark night of the soul," as John of the Cross will describe it in a couple of centuries to come.

Rumi: Indeed, we often hear mystics talking of dying to one's self so as to live in God and God live in the individual. It seems ironic, that, as we become less and less, we actually become more and more because God lives in us more and more. I called it an irony in human terms, but it is reality—or Reality. The Apostle Paul, himself a mystic, expressed it as: "I live no longer, not I, but Christ lives in me."[2] Indeed, for me and other Sufis, we view Jesus as the ultimate model of self-perishing, whose example we should emulate.

Eckhart: Interesting comment, Mevlana. For many of us Christians, Jesus was, as Marcus Borg will write long after us, "the decisive revelation of God's character and passion." The insights of mysticism proffer a remarkable dynamism to this thought of Borg's.[3]

Borg also will note that, just as Christians understand the decisive revelation of God and life with God in Jesus, Jews find God's decisive revelation in the Torah; and Muslims believe the Qur'an to be God's decisive revelation; and Muhammad, God's final prophet.[4]

Of course, as we have remarked throughout the night, we notice God's self-revealing in everyone, and a clearer, brighter self-revealing in people who are prophets or doers of good deeds, whether they perform enormous endeavors in the human panorama or attend to the "smaller" acts of grace in everyday life.

For me, "the noblest and most extraordinary of all events (the birth of the divine Son in the soul) is the most common (in any act of justice, insofar as it is just)."[5] Mysticism and justice are interrelated, and a person cannot achieve the completeness of one without the other.

Rumi: I am in total accord. In fact, as I mentioned earlier, I have at times seen myself as a "slave" in carrying out actions of service with the joy of adoration. I want to be the Beloved's hands, feet, and mouth.

De León: I would speak to another point for those in the 21st century. One paradox in experiencing mystical union is that, no matter how intense or ecstatic, it generally does not last long in terms of human time, although, when experienced, there is no sense of time.

Some spiritual writers postulate that the experience of mystical union may actually take place within a nano-second or two. Yet, to the mystic it is an experience of eternity, without, and outside, time, and leaves the person even more hungry and thirsty for further union with the Divine.

You have expressed this timelessness paradox lyrically, Meister Eckhart: "The now wherein God made the world is as near this time as the now I am speaking in this moment, and the last day is as near this now as was yesterday."[6]

I also appreciate how Rabbi Heschel will portray the mystical union quite poetically: "A moment comes like a thunderbolt in which a flash of the undisclosed rends our dark apathy asunder. The ineffable has shuddered itself into the soul. It has entered our consciousness like a ray of light passing into a lake."[7]

Rumi: Ah, Rabbi Heschel eloquent and fervent, as always. One of our later Sufi scholars, Ibrahim Syed, will describe it this way: "The mystical experience is a transient, extraordinary experience marked by feelings of being in unity, harmonious relationship to the Divine and everything in existence, as well as euphoric feelings, loss of ego functioning, alterations in time and space perception, and the sense of lacking control over the event."[8]

Eckhart: An interesting example of mysticism's transient nature is the Gospel narrative of Jesus' transfiguration.[9] Jesus takes the apostles James, John, and Peter up a mountain and becomes transfigured before them, "his face shining as the sun; and his garments, white as the light." Immediately and suddenly standing with him are Moses and Elijah, all conversing together.

As Moses and Elijah begin to recede from view, Peter asks Jesus if they should set up tents, dwelling places, for the three. Just then a bright cloud overshadows them and a "voice" says, "This is my Son, whom I love; listen to him." The disciples prostrate themselves in fear, but Jesus touches them and tells them not to be afraid.

When the disciples "look up," Jesus is standing alone; Moses and Elijah have vanished. As they return down the mountain, Jesus tells the disciples not to tell anyone "the things they have seen" until the Human One is raised up.

The Gospel texts are clear that the mountain's "location" is mythical, a place beyond place and a time out of time. This story has various theological interpretations and is a literary parallel with Moses' transfiguration on Mount Sinai and Elijah's encounter with God in the sound of sheer silence on Mount Horeb.

This story is a paradigm of mystical transiency, indicated by Peter's desire to pitch the three tents to capture the moment, to hold on to it, if possible. But the nature of mystical union is that it cannot be contained or controlled in time and place. They "go back down" the mountain, that extra-ordinary place set apart. The four of them return back through the thin veil, and on into their daily lives, having had an ineffable experience of radical amazement that transfigured them each in different ways and changed their lives.

An encounter with the Divine on a mountain transformed Moses, and the "work" of his transformation was to return to Egypt and bring liberation to his people. Jesus "repented" (literally, "returned") to his authentic God-self in the baptismal waters of the Jordan River; but his real vocation was an "anointing" to inaugurate the year of Jubilee by bringing good news to the poor, proclaiming release to the captives and recovery of sight to the blind, and helping the oppressed go free.[10]

Rumi: The Prophet Muhammad's life changed at age 40 when the angel Gabriel visited him in a cave. Shortly after that, as a result of his mystical experience, he began preaching his revelations publicly, that God is One and complete surrender to God is the only way.

De León: I really appreciate these deeper interpretations of events on our traditions, which reflect a mystical meaning that people too often overlook.

Eckhart: If I may slightly shift the discussion, esteemed Colleagues. From my perspective, one of the hurdles in Christian mystical experience has been in communicating a discipline or method for it to people generally, such as there came to be in Zen or Tibetan mysticism and the mysticism of Islam and Judaism. I am partly to blame for this since I did not generally preach my sermons in any organized or thematic way. Then, in course, the church authorities came down on me ruthlessly and generally buried my work for a few centuries.

I am happy, however, to foresee the development of "centering prayer," a form of contemplative prayer, in the 20th and 21st centuries. Thomas Keating, a Trappist monk, will do much to help make centering prayer and mystical experience more accessible to everyday people. This was always my goal in teaching, and why I spoke German, the language of the people, in my Sunday sermons, to reach all the people, rather than only write Latin tomes for the theologians.

For me, it has always been a priority to reach people in their "everydayness" since everyone can be a mystic. In fact, Thomas Merton, one of the 20th century's most respected spiritual writers, realized this moved fairly dramatically from living an isolated monastic life to one of more intense involvement with the world, and even seemed to bemoan being somewhat late to the scene.[11]

Rumi: Yes, you are correct, Meister Eckhart. It is clear to me that mysticism is for everyone; and there should be no dichotomy between the cloister and the day-to-day work of every person. Indeed, in my view, mysticism is an essential aspect of everyday life.

And one of the ways in which we come to know the Beloved is in creation around us. Thus, the more we labor to improve creation, the more we are a partner with God in helping creation manifest God further; and, thus, we know the Beloved better. I would emphasize that struggling to improve creation includes bettering the lives of those around us so that God is manifest more brightly in them, for us to see and be in union with. The reciprocal nature of the exchange between self and creation is like an upward spiral, bringing us closer and closer to God, which, of course, is what mysticism is about.

De León: I absolutely agree, Meister Eckhart and Mevlana, totally and without reserve. I would only add one caveat, namely, that one who follows this mystical path needs to do so carefully, step-by-step. Discipline and guidance are critical. To that end, I suggest strongly that each person look for another individual with experience to help be a guide forward.

Fortunately, this will become an increasingly easier endeavor in the 21st century. There will be an impressive array of excellent books, videos, and publications available. In many communities, there are local meetings of kindred folks; and everywhere there are many with experience who can be spiritual advisors and companions.

So, too, one's religious tradition may be extremely helpful, not as an end in itself, but as a background to help us move along to the point where we take the next step past religious tradition and into being ready for union with the Divine or however we want to name it. We know, of course, that we eventually have to un-name it and be enfolded with the power and presence that has no name or description.

In fact, ritual practices, prayers, and narratives of the past may take on different and deeper meaning as one moves toward great mystical union, just like the stories of Adam and Eve, Moses on the mountain, and Jesus' transfiguration have done this for us.

Eckhart: And, speaking of stories, my dear Mevlana, I love your brilliant and stirring story about Moses' encounter with the shepherd. Moses comes upon a shepherd speaking to God in earthy terms—combing God's hair, fixing God's shoes, and so on. Moses chastises him for speaking to God in such an earthy, mundane way.

Later, in an intense mystical experience, God rebukes Moses for his arrogance in thinking he knows how to love God better than the shepherd. Moses then runs after the shepherd to apologize; but instead the shepherd thanks and blesses Moses for scolding him and "applying the whip" to his horse so that it "jumped out of itself" and "the divine nature and my human nature came together."[12]

Both Moses and the shepherd grew closer to God. Moses had seen himself only as the shepherd's spiritual guide; but, in reality, their interaction caused both of them to grow.

De León: Gentlemen, I would add a related intervention on this point. The masters and teachers talk about a three-fold challenge in mysticism across traditions: how to get there; how to get back from there; and how to communicate what has happened. Meeting and understanding this triple challenge is critical because of the real possibility of going mad or even dying, if one is not properly prepared, so profoundly intense is the experience.

Sometimes mystical experiences are like embracing fire. As Kabbalah scholar Daniel Matt will write:

> Mystical teachings are enticing, powerful, and potentially dangerous. The spiritual seeker soon discovers that he or she is not exploring something "up there," but rather the beyond that lies within. Letting go of traditional notions of God and self can be both liberating and terrifying. [13]

People can have great difficulty, if they feel an inability to experience the ineffability of the Divine or, if they do, a "let down" when they return to daily life, which appears even more banal and problematic than before. We know of a similar phenomenon where people experience life so deeply that they cannot cope with all its pain and sorrow and take their life.

This is why it is so critical to have a spiritual guide or advisor, someone, who is already on the path, to avoid any of the dangers or pitfalls of mystical practice and, of course, to help sweep litter off the pathway or offer a directional signal to the extent possible.

Rumi: Rabbi, you could not have said it better. I have been through this, and, on occasions, my family and friends thought I had gone mad. I have even found myself whirling and dancing about, sometimes in blissful euphoria or in profound grief. Mystical union is powerful, actually indescribable, and, every so often, extraordinarily ecstatic.

One of the times I went nearly mad, and spun about and danced crazily, was when my spiritual mentor and soul-mate, Shams, disappeared from my life. I even left Konya and went searching for him, all the way to Damascus. While on the way there, I had a mystical awakening and realized:

> Why am I seeking? I am the same as He.
> His essence speaks through me.
> I have been looking for myself! [14]

Eckhart: What an exquisite twist of history, Mevlana! The Apostle Paul also had a mystical awakening on the way to Damascus, with a vision of Jesus. How fitting you were both going to the same location, albeit by different routes, but ended up in the same spiritual place—an encounter with the

Sacred which is what the journey of mysticism is all about—"many paths to the same city," so to speak.

De León: An apt observation, Meister Eckhart. You know, dear Brothers, turning the discussion a bit, there will be a good deal of talk in the late 20th and early 21st centuries about self-awareness and self-development, and hundreds of books written on these themes. Sometimes, though, I fear it stops there and becomes an end unto itself.

Eckhart: Yes, Rabbi Moses, that is accurate. Developing the self is a worthy project, and even required, but only because it means the individual then has more of a rich and abounding personal character to give to God and to others, and to "channel" God. It is like remodeling the well to the Underground River to make it sturdier and more efficient from which to draw water rumbling below.

Rumi: To become holy or worthy of the Beloved, one must die to self, and live for God only, with the mysteries of the Divine always before our eyes and on our lips. To die to self requires enormous self-discipline, a process that may require one to endure physical and emotional pain. I recall, Meister Eckhart, that Jesus used similar language of dying to one's self in order to be born again.

I am not referring to practices of bodily mortification and excessive self-denial in and of themselves, which was the practice for centuries. Not only can this have serious health consequences, but it has the inherent danger of causing ego-building (a potential for ego-centered heroism), instead of being ego-diminishing, which is necessary to receive the Beloved.

I sometimes refer to the individual person as a vessel into which Divine Love is poured. The more spacious and refined the vessel, the more it is recipient of Divine Love and the more gifts the person has to give to the community around him or her. On the other hand, if the vessel is cluttered and filled with ego material, it leaves no room for Godness and God's presence. Discipline and self-denial must be tied to making our vessel bigger and better, not to strengthening one's ego with a self-defeating sense of personal willpower. We need to be filled with Godness so as to be a conduit of God.

Eckhart: Yes, another way of expressing this receptivity to God or passivity is that God is not in the business of leave-taking; we are. When we go out of ourselves to find God or fetch God we are making a mistake. We do not find God outside ourselves; and we should not conceive God except as in us, and in us as the vessels we are. As I emphasized in my sermons, "To be full of things is to be empty of God. To be empty of things is to be full of God."

Teresa of Avila will be fond of saying, "If the host would prepare the house, there is no doubt the Guest will come."[15] We sometimes call this self-abandonment; the Beguines more erotically talk of the soul's nakedness and God's ravishing.

Rumi: Of course, no matter how well we finely hone the vessel, there is always a veil between us and the Beloved, a veil that we want to pierce, push aside, or even peer through. The thinner the veil—the less self—the closer we are to the Beloved. But the veil (ego) is always there, however thin. This may pain us, but it also gives us joy and hope because it means we are ever closer to melding into the Divine Lover, much like Moses seeing a glimpse of God's back on Mount Sinai.

De León: The vessel analogy is fascinating, Mevlana, because we have a similar metaphor in the Kabbalah: If we are attached to the material nature of the world, if we think of ourselves as something, then God cannot be clothed in us, for God is infinite. No vessel can contain God, unless we think of ourselves as *Eyn* ("nothing"). We must remove ourselves from the material aspects of things so that the Divine may dwell in us.

Eckhart: As to this vessel analogy, which is rich, the Apostle Paul, in a mystical reflection, reminds us that we ourselves do not make the vessel more spacious and receptive to the outpouring of God alone, but that God does this work in us and *with us*. *God* prepares us, not just we ourselves.

Paul points out that we are but vessels of clay, earthen vessels, but made so that God may show God's glory.[16] It is imperative that we have this humility or surrender in mind as we do the work with God in making our vessels more receptive to the Divine. If not, we slip into an "I can do it myself" mode, which only stiffens the barrier to the Holy One, instead of diminishing it. Or, as you would say, Rabbi Moses, drives God further from our awareness.

Rumi: Yes, our task is not to search for love, but to seek and remove the barriers within ourselves that we have built against it. We Sufis also use another metaphor, a mirror. The more cloudy and opaque the mirror, the more dimly we see the Beloved, and the more dimly is the Beloved seen in us. In a totally clear and clean mirror, the mirror disappears in the sense that the image becomes one with the person reflected in the mirror. As one of my poems expresses it, "You cannot see yourself without a mirror. Look at the Beloved, he is the brightest mirror."

De León: What strikes me about the vessel and mirror analogies is the ultimate paradox of mysticism, that the more we slough off our ego construct (with God's help, of course), the greater is the self-manifestation of God in us, and the greater our own authenticity. In other words, it is not me doing good deeds, but God doing good in and through me.

I respectfully would like to mention another of your poems, Mevlana, if I may. I know we are quoting your verse a good deal in our conversation tonight, but poetry is so succinct and expresses in so few words what others write pages and pages about—and you do it so well:

Knock, and he will open the door.
Vanish, and he will make you shine like the sun.
Fall, and he will raise you to the heavens.
Become nothing, and he will turn you into everything.

Getting over our self-centeredness and surrendering is such a critical and difficult task, especially when our social and economic constructs fiercely reinforce self-centeredness and drum it into our souls. But it is such a self-defeating scheme, both for the individual and for society as a whole.

Rumi: Yes, so true, sadly. Indeed, one of the sweet ironies of what we are discussing this evening is that, as I have penned elsewhere, "embarking on the Journey of Love takes you from yourself to your self."

Eckhart: You know, Friends, on another point about our self-centeredness, we too often tend to view and describe ourselves as part of the universe. But that is inaccurate. We are not just part of the universe as kind of an object of creation. The universe is in us, and we partially inhabit the universe, and vice versa. God is immanent, totally present, and transcendent in the universe. That means we are part of everyone else, and everyone is part of us, past, present, and to come. In a real sense, we are wrapped in one cosmic Unity.

You expressed it succinctly, Mevlana, in another of your poetic insights: "You are not a drop in the ocean. You are the entire ocean in a drop." This reminds me of what German aphorist Georg Christoph Lichtenberg will write in the 18th century, "In each of us, there is a little of all of us."

So profound is this understanding and the love it engenders that, when we empty our vessel of our ego-constructs and distractions, love is powerful enough to change the course of history and mold the world into what it—*we*—should become. Or, as Teilhard de Chardin will say a few centuries hence: "Once we discover love, we will have discovered fire a second time"; I pray every day that "you set me on fire to do your will and have no ego."[17]

Rumi: In other words, as you so eloquently expressed it, Meister Eckhart, we should love everyone, especially those on the margins of society because of the Godness in them.

As you mentioned earlier, we must support others and become activists for them. This includes doing acts of charity, like volunteering in a food pantry, which is good and necessary; but we also must commit ourselves to the hard task of changing social structures that cause poverty and drive us to war. This might entail political involvement and community organizing. Striving for justice and peace is always the result of union with the Lover.

We Sufis have the practice of trying to envisage the person to whom we are speaking as surrounded and embraced by the Divine Lover, and we hope that person feels or observes the Beloved surrounding us, and thus all of us enfolded together in the Lover's arms. I once used another way of expressing this sentiment:

> Borrow the Beloved's eyes.
> Look through them, and you will see
> the Beloved's face.

Unfortunately, as the great American singer Pearl Bailey will express it, "People see God every day, but they just don't recognize him."

De León: It strikes me that this may all sound nice and pleasant when we say it; but what is important—and what we some sometimes overlook—is that being in the Mystery of mysticism entails great personal discipline. But there is also "positive" discipline involved, besides the ascetical, and that involves good companionship, upright character, attending to music and poetry that helps lead to ecstasy, good counseling, and prophet-ship or leadership.[18] Or, in a happenstance like Siddhartha's, listening to a saint under a tree.

Rumi: Yes, Meister Eckhart, very important points! I once found myself saying to someone seeking my counsel, "Set your life on fire. Seek those who fan your flames."

De León: Mevlana, you use such expressive verse! As for me, my experience is that we cannot travel to where we long to go without consistent spiritual and physical practices, such as fasting and a meditation regime. You wrote it well, or "channeled" it well, as you would prefer to say, Mevlana, in another striking poem:

> Do not avoid discipline.
> You have learned ways to make a living
> for your body. Now learn to support
> your soul. You wear fine clothing.
> How do you dress your spirit?

Eckhart: I think one reason that religious traditions of the East, like Buddhism or Hinduism, are attractive to people is they provide contemplative methods without the baggage that organized religion in the West has accumulated. Although that baggage can be heavy, I do think people can put it behind them with some effort and find guidance in Western religious traditions. Nor is there any reason that practices of Eastern mysticism cannot be incorporated into other belief systems, as well.

It always has been useful for me to get away for a week or so and be alone with God. Making quiet time is a form of ascetic practice; and it should be done every day, regularly. Sometimes, I have found it helpful to recite some poetry or do spiritual reading to get me focused,[19] and then move into contemplation, removing myself from myself as much as possible so as to let

God enter in and take over. Mornings, the beginning of the day, seems to be a good time for many people to do this.

It just occurred to me, Mevlana, that you have some practical and pithy verse about the kinds of ascetic practices you favor, which seem fairly universal:

> I will for you
> to have a fear of god, secretly and openly,
> to eat less,
> to speak less,
> to refrain from sins,
> to continue fasting and praying,
> to abstain always from lust,
> to endure people's torment and ill-treatment,
> to avoid being with dissolute and ordinary people,
> to be kind and wise with people.
> For, the most beneficial person
> is the one who does a favor for others.
> And the most beneficial word
> is the one which is short and sincere. [20]

Rumi: I gently remind you, fellow Companions, that yoga and dance also can be excellent ascetic and contemplative practices.

De León: For my own spiritual practice, I try to retire to the desert areas or woods of al-Ándalus when I can, at least every month, and spend some time quietly contemplating the Divine Mystery—centering prayer, as it will come to be known. The important thing is to have sacred time and space to withdraw from the all-consuming frenzy of daily existence. We each need to carve out a quiet period every day, dedicated to reflection and prayer. And we should build into our lives longer stretches of calm with some regularity to excuse ourselves from life's tumult spinning about us.

Eckhart: Good point, Rabbi Moses. I also find it valuable to sneak away in a secluded place, perhaps even attend an organized or silent retreat. The future United States will have retreat facilities of all kinds all across the country. One can easily find a retreat center that speaks to one's needs and traditions or customs. For those who like to travel, there is nothing comparable to the Taizé Community in France. It is a remarkable ecumenical community that attracts young people from around the globe. [21]

I also would mention the 12-Step programs that will develop in the mid-20th century. They will have their origins for people with chemical or substance addictions, but will expand into other areas, such as relational matters. These programs' strong spiritual underpinnings dovetail quite suitably with the kind of mysticism we have been discussing this evening. [22]

Rumi: Ahem, Gentlemen, I again would like to put in a good word for dance and yoga.

De León: Ah, yes, Mevlana. Thanks for the reminder. And people say I am a character? They have not met you is all I can tell them.

Rumi: Ha, ha, Rabbi. But, seriously, sometimes, when I talk about dance as prayerful or contemplative, there comes to mind the famous quote of Friedrich Nietzsche, the German philosopher who will follow after us in the late 19th century, speaking through Zarathustra, a namesake for the Persian founder of Zoroastrianism:

> I would only believe in a god who could dance. And when I saw my devil I found him serious, thorough, profound, and solemn: it was the spirit of gravity—through him all things fall. Not by wrath does one kill but by laughter. Come, let us kill the spirit of gravity![23]

Eckhart: This, interestingly enough, reminds me, Mevlana, of yet another poem of yours about crafting ourselves to be worthy vessels of the Divine, something we discussed earlier in the evening:

> Every moment,
> I shape my destiny
> With a chisel—
> I am the carpenter of my own soul.[24]

De León: Such an apropos metaphor, Mevlana. Good job!

If I may, Gentlemen, I fear that, as society develops more, there will be fewer opportunities for tranquil spaces and silent periods in one's daily routine. In fact, people who join the planet after us in the 21st century will find themselves deluged with social media and the pressing urge to be in constant contact with it. I would imagine part of their ascetic practice will be learning self-discipline to stand back from all that pervasive distraction, let it go for periods of time, and enter into a peaceful mode to hear and receive the Divine.[25]

You have expressed this so delightfully, Mevlana:

> How could the soul not take flight,
> when from the glorious Presence,
> a soft call flows sweet as honey,
> comes right up to her
> and whispers, "Rise up now, come away"?
> How could the fish not jump
> immediately from dry land into water,
> when the sound of the water from the ocean
> of fresh waves springs to his ears?

Rumi: Speaking of social media, Rabbi, some very helpful aspects of it will have appeared by the 21st century. For example, one can find all sorts of resources that provide guidance and assistance, such as YouTube and Face-book pages, and even some that offer daily contemplative meditations.[26]

Altogether, I would conclude my thoughts on this part of our dialog with my version of the "Golden Rule": "The way you make love / Is the way God will be with you." This refers not only to the love between a person and the Beloved, but also how we love others, that is, how we actually "make" love in our relationships with each other. Paul McCartney someday will sing a beautiful lyrical song, equating the love one takes with the love one makes.[27]

Eckhart: Well said, Mevlana. That leaves me also with one last point to close out this particular theme, one not as upbeat, but grounded in historical reality; it can be dangerous to be a mystic. We talked earlier about the internal danger, not being able to disengage from mystical experience, and the necessity of guidance. But there is also a social peril, which could be isolation, hatred, imprisonment, and even death.

We have already discussed the Inquisition burning Marguerite Porete at the stake. Rome executed Paul the Apostle by the sword. Buddha survived several assassination attempts. Dr. King will be gunned down during a sanitation workers' strike he is supporting in Memphis.

This is because, as Philip Simmons will write, "Mystical seeing exalts us at the same time as it knocks us out of our complacency, our confidence, our righteousness. (That's why true mystics have so often been labeled trouble-makers and heretics: they refuse the comforts of orthodoxy.) . . . . The mystic, like the poet, like all of us who seek the fullest apprehension of life, must leave the settled world of the known to dwell in the wilderness of mystery."[28] It is also the wilderness of freedom. Simmons' book, *Learning to Fall: The Blessings of an Imperfect Life*, will become popular in the 21st century as an expression of "everyday" mysticism that drew from all traditions. He will author it after learning he had ALS, or Lou Gehrig's disease.

De León: That was a superb quotation from Simmons. As we spoke earlier, charitable works are important doings of God, but so is effecting justice and social change. Sometimes, the mystic's prophetic message is too strong for the powers that be, and they feel compelled to rid themselves of the troublesome meddler. This is as true of those whom we consider to be leaders, as it is for common folk. It is almost as if the authorities become unhinged with the mystics' message of radical freedom and justice.

Rumi: I am reminded of *The Grand Inquisitor*, that powerful parable, which Fyodor Dostoevsky will incorporate in his 19th-century novel *The Brothers Karamazov*,[29] that Ivan, a materialist and atheist, relates to his brother Alyosha, a young Christian mystic.

A man in Seville, whom people recognize as Jesus, returned to earth after fifteen centuries, has been healing people, preaching, and moving "silently in their midst with a gentle smile of infinite compassion," as he did when first on earth.

After witnessing Jesus raise a young girl from the dead after her funeral, the Grand Inquisitor, who is also the Cardinal of Seville and who had 100 people burned at the stake as "wicked heretics" the day before in an auto-da-fé spectacle for the city, arrests Jesus and sentences him to death as the townsfolk cower in fear. For the Cardinal, Jesus was a dangerous trouble-maker.

During the night, the Grand Inquisitor secretly visits him, acknowledging that he is Jesus. The Inquisitor then engages in a powerful monologue about human nature and freedom, and its fundamental ambiguity. He argues it was necessary for the Church to become what it became because people cannot handle the radical freedom that Jesus proclaimed about his mystical vision of society.

The Inquisitor's soliloquy is essentially "I know you are Jesus; but you are messing up the church, which is why we have to kill you." Eventually, there is an ambiguous ending, when Jesus kisses the Grand Inquisitor, who allows Jesus to leave by the alleyway. This parable could easily apply to the Beguines and Beghards, who tried to live as did Jesus, but, because they challenged the status quo, met opposition from church authorities, sometimes fiercely so.

De León: You know, Mevlana, this chilling fable reminds me of how Morpheus will express a similar idea in the 1999 allegorical movie *The Matrix*: "You have to understand, most of these people are not ready to be unplugged. And many of them are so inured, so hopelessly dependent on the system that they will fight to protect it."[30]

Somewhat different from the Dostoevsky tale, the "townsfolk" in *The Matrix* (or current society) might not, or will not, even recognize Jesus; but the result is the same. Everyone in the system from top to bottom, not just the powers-that-be, will fight desperately to maintain the system to which they have attached themselves, and vice versa. They and their institutions are all agents of socialization, one might say, that resist change. They fear freedom.

Eckhart: Thank you, Rabbi, for reminding us of The *Matrix*. Jackson Browne will have a haunting prophetic song "The Rebel Jesus" about this same theme in the modern era, that it is one thing to help out the poor a little, but quite another to interfere with the structural reasons that cause people to be poor. Those who meddle, he says, will end up the same as did Jesus.[31]

So, I would wrap up with two sobering thoughts. First, the personal practice of mysticism can be painstaking in learning to become a better vessel for the Divine; second, the practice of mysticism in the community, the work of justice, is equally painstaking, and sometimes perilous. But, all in all, there is no better way to be than to *be*.

Jesus said, blessed are those who suffer hatred, revilement, persecution, and even death, for theirs is the kingdom. I suspect he would also add, "Blessed are you, the mystic, for you are in the kingdom."

NOTES

1. See "A Voice in the Wind," July 24, 2012, http://avoiceinthewind.blogspot.com/2006/07/evening-with-rumi.html.

2. Galatians 2:20.

3. See Marcus J. Borg, "Yes and No" and "Mystical Experiences of God," http://www.marcusjborg.com/.

4. Marcus J. Borg, *Jesus: The Life, Teachings, and Relevance of a Religious Revolutionary* (New York: HarperOne, 2008), Chap. 1.

5. Michael A. Sells, *Mystical Languages of Unsaying* (Chicago: University of Chicago, 1994), 7–8.

6. F. C. Happold, *Mysticism* (New York: Penguin Books, 1970), 279 (Meister Eckhart, Sermon LXXXIV).

7. Abraham Joshua Heschel, *Man Is Not Alone: A Philosophy of Religion* (New York: Farrar, Straus and Giroux Publishers, 1976), 78–79.

8. Ibrahim B. Syed, *Islamic Research Foundation International, Inc.*, "Sufism and Neurotheology," www.irfi.org.

9. See Matthew 17:1–9; Mark 9:2-8; Luke 9:28–36; and 2 Peter 1:16–18.

10. Luke 4:18.

11. See Thomas Merton, *Conjectures of a Guilty Bystander* (Colorado Springs, CO; Image Books, 1968).

12. Farkato, "Moses Heard a Shepherd on the Road Praying," Sept. 21, 2011, https://www.youtube.com/watch?v=IKU49slrb38; Ehsan, "Moses and the Shepherd (Rumi)," June 16, 2003, http://www.shiachat.com/forum/topic/12060-moses-and-the-shepherd-rumi/.

13. Daniel C. Matt, *Scholars Press*, 1982 "Introduction to the Essential Kabbalah." portfolio.du.edu/downloadItem/221662.

14. *The Essential Rumi*, trans. Coleman Barks and John Moyne (New York: HarperOne, 2004), xx.

15. Wayne Teasdale, *The Mystic Hours: A Daybook of Inspirational Wisdom and Devotion* (Novato, CA: New World Library, 2004), 9.

16. 2 Corinthians 4:7

17. Pierre Teilhard de Chardin, "The Evolution of Chastity," *Toward the Future* (Boston, MA: Mariner Books, 2002), chap. XI.

18. Ori Z. Soltes, *Mysticism in Judaism, Christianity, and Islam: Searching for Oneness* (Lanham, MD: Rowman & Littlefield, 2009), 91, 99–100. Soltes notes that a prophet is a saint and a *Logos* ("Word") of God, who manifests God's word and articulates it to humanity.

19. There is any number of accessible short daily meditation books, compiled from the writings of various mystics, available. See, e.g., *Words to Live By: Short Readings of Daily Wisdom*, ed. Eknath Easwaran (Tomales, CA; Nilgiri Press, 2010); *A Year with Rumi: Daily Readings*, ed. Coleman Barks (New York: HarperOne, 2006); Wayne Teasdale, *The Mystic Hours*; John Kirvan, *God Hunger: Discovering the Mystic in All of Us* (Notre Dame, IN: Sorin Books, 1999); *The Mystic Vision: Daily Encounters with the Divine*, eds. Anne Baring and Andrew Harvey (London: Godsfield Press Ltd, 1995); John Kirvan, The 30 Days with a Great Spiritual Teacher Series, 8 books (https://www.avemariapress.com/series/6/The-30-Days-with-a-Great-Spiritual-Teacher-Series/). As already indicated, YouTube has numerous offerings of readings and presentations suitable for daily reflection; and various sources offer daily meditations by e-mail.

20. Bismillahir Rahmanir Rahim, "His Will," *Mevlana Rumi*, Feb. 21, 2007, http://mevlana-rumi.blogspot.com/2007_02_01_archive.html.

21. The Taizé Community, an ecumenical monastic order in Taizé, France, has more than one hundred brothers from about thirty countries across the world, from both Protestant and Catholic traditions. See "The Taizé Community," http://www.taize.fr/en_rubrique8.html.

22. Rami Shapiro, *Recovery—The Sacred Art: The Twelve Steps as Spiritual Practice* (Woodstock, VT: SkyLight Paths Publishing, 2009); Rebecca Clay, "The Secret of the 12 steps: Researchers Explore Spirituality's Role in Substance Abuse Prevention and Treatment," *American Psychological Association*, Dec. 2003, http://www.apa.org/monitor/dec03/secret.aspx.

23. Friedrich Nietzsche, *Thus Spake Zarathustra: A Book for All and None*, trans. Thomas Common, http://www.gutenberg.org/files/1998/1998-h/1998-h.htm.

24. See Llewellyn Vaughan-Lee, *Prayer of the Heart in Christian and Sufi Mysticism* (Point Reyes Station, CA; Golden Sufi Center, 2012).

25. David Ariel, *Mystic Quest: An Introduction to Jewish Mysticism* (New York: Schocken Books, 1992).

26. See, e.g., Center for Action and Contemplation, https://cac.org/; "Rumi's Largest Page on Facebook," https://www.facebook.com/mevlana?fref=photo; Robert Kyr, "The Cloud of Unknowing: Songs of the Soul," *Allmusic*, http://www.allmusic.com/album/MW0002693078.

27. Kallilms, July 25, 2007, "The Beatles-The End," https://www.youtube.com/watch?v=cWNsdBfGacA.

28. Philip Simmons, *Learning to Fall: The Blessings of an Imperfect Life* (New York: Bantam Books, 2002), 102.

29. Fyodor Dostoevsky, *Grand Inquisitor* (Milestones of Thought) (New York: Bloomsbury Academic, 1981). For text, see "The Grand Inquisitor," trans. H.P. Blavatsky, Gutenberg Project, June 28, 2010, http://www.gutenberg.org/files/8578/8578-h/8578-h.htm (text).

30. "They Will Fight to Protect the Matrix by Greg Calise," *Riverbank of Truth*, Aug. 28, 2013, http://riverbankoftruth.com/2013/08/28/they-will-fight-to-protect-the-matrix-by-greg-calise/.

31. See Jackson Browne, *Metrolyrics*, "The Rebel Jesus," http://www.metrolyrics.com/the-rebel-jesus-lyrics-jackson-browne.html.

Chapter Thirteen

They Conclude—
the Underground River
and Expanding the Circle

May the Warm Winds of Heaven
Blow softly upon your house.
May the Great Spirit
Bless all who enter there.
May your Moccasins
Make happy tracks
In many snows.
And may the Rainbow
Always touch your shoulder.

—Cherokee Blessing

Rumi: Well, dear Brothers, it looks as if our conversation has drawn to conclusion as daybreak arrives. It is hard to believe we have talked through the night, but it has been an exceptional pleasure. Dawn is close, and soon I must meet some Muslim friends for morning prayer. I believe you both also have plans to meet with other friends and colleagues today and take advantage of being here in scenic Venice.

De León: An agreeable pleasure, indeed. As we share these freshly-baked cinnamon rolls the innkeeper kindly has provided us, perhaps we might make a round of concluding observations to wrap up our wonderful time together.

Rumi: Very well, Rabbi Moses. For my part, mystics, as our particular talks have revealed, commonly refer to descriptive metaphors, like romantic love, expanding the circle, and the Underground River. In that regard, I would like to offer a poem by the great Sufi mystic Ibn al-'Arabi, who

143

originally hails from your area of the world, Rabbi, and with whom I spent
some valuable time in Damascus:

> My heart can take on any form:
> a meadow for gazelles,
> a cloister for monks,
> for the idols, sacred ground,
> Ka'ba for the circling pilgrim,
> the tables of the Torah,
> the scrolls of the Quran.
>
> My creed is Love;
> wherever its caravan turns along the way,
> that is my belief,
> my faith. [1]

De León: Beautiful, Mevlana, and right on target! Thomas Keating,
whom we mentioned earlier, will analogize the spokes of a wheel to make the
same point. As the spokes get closer to the center of the wheel, they get
closer to each other and to God. [2] They never become one, but they get to the
same place. That is certainly true of us, I dare say. The further out the spokes
extend, the more expansive the wheel and its circle. I hope our comments
will help expand the circle of mystical experience, as it were, so that more
people find themselves included within it.

Eckhart: It has been thought-provoking to me, as we have talked, to
recognize the roots of our spiritual interconnectedness in a way I had not
considered before. Much of the connection appears to come through al-
Ándalus, curiously enough. Kabbalistic thought likely began in the Middle
East and migrated to Cologne; and then it relocated to Provence, through
Isaac the Blind, the "Father of Kabbalah." From there, it became anchored in
al-Ándalus, thanks in large part to you, Rabbi Moses.

Then, we have Ibn al-'Arabi, perhaps the most preeminent Sufi master,
who lived in al-Ándalus and studied Kabbalah and Christian thought. He
eventually moved to Damascus for the remaining years of his life, and you,
Mevlana, were there in Damascus for the last four of those years. That is a
tribute to the richness of life that graced the southern region of the Iberian
Peninsula during the 500 years when Jewish, Christian, and Islamic thought
and culture co-existed and learned from each other. Our lives are all so much
better for it.

Rumi: Professor Michael Sells will suggest in the 20th century that we
three may be living in the historical culmination of the larger Abrahamic and
Graeco-Roman "metaculture" and that doctrinal differences in our religions
put in "high relief" what happens with apophatic thinking, that it gets us to
common ground. [3]

De León: Well, we would not disabuse Professor Sells of his valuable insight. Mysticism is everywhere. There are indeed many wells, among all people and in all religions, even while each tradition cloaks the mystical union experience within its own history, ritual, mythology, and even geography.

Mystical union is distinctive and specific to one's own tradition and experience. Yet, while each experience is unique, it is also inherently universal. Philip Simmons, a wonderful late 20th-century writer on "everyday" mysticism, will express it eloquently: "Only in the mystic vision, or death, do we enter in . . . the sacred circle at whose center God lies . . . . [E]ach of the world's religions teaches its own way of getting [home] . . . ."[4]

I would like to wrap up my thoughts by paraphrasing how Professor Sells will conclude his book *Mystical Languages of Unsaying*. Mysticism of the unsaying, apophatic kind, is

> . . . not an easy task. Its achievement is unstable and fleeting. It demands a rigorous and sustained effort both to use and free oneself from normal habits of thought and expression. It demands a willingness to let go, at a particular moment, of the grasping for guarantees and for knowledge as a possession. It demands a moment of vulnerability. Yet for those who value it, this moment . . . is what it is to be human.[5]

Eckhart: What an evocative summary, Rabbi! Thank you so much. For my part, I return to my analogy of wells, drawing from the mighty Underground River that no one can dam up and no one can stop. I am reminded, Mevlana, of two other of your sayings: "Go to the well of deep Love inside each of us" and "I drank water from your spring, and felt the current take me."

We have drawn, it seems, from our respective wells, and tasted the sweet, cool freshness of drinking from the Underground River, each in our own way.

Rumi: Yes, Meister Eckhart, we have felt the current lift and carry us. Gentlemen, it has been a profound honor to have met you both. I am richer for our night-long sharing of thoughts, and the Beloved feels closer to me because of our communion.

Farewell, Good Friends. Let's hope the reader has benefited from our conversation that our 21st-century interlocutors have tried to narrate. I offer you my peace and love, and a hearty embrace. To quote the future mystic Evelyn Underhill, "The note we end on is, and must be, the note of inexhaustible possibility and hope."[6]

NOTES

1. See Jamil Hussain, *Vimeo*, "Wonder! [Words of Ibn Arabi]," http://vimeo.com/12236444.

2. Thomas Keating, *The Better Part: Stages of Contemplative Living* (New York: Bloomsbury Academic, 2007), 107.

3. Michael A. Sells, *Mystical Languages of Unsaying* (Chicago: University of Chicago, 1994), 206.

4. Philip Simmons, *Learning to Fall: The Blessings of an Imperfect Life* (New York: Bantam Books, 2002), 91, 133.

5. Sells, *Mystical Languages of Unsaying*, 217.

6. Evelyn Underwood, quoted in John Kirvan, *God Hunger: Discovering the Mystic in All of Us* (Notre Dame, IN: Sorin Books, 1999), 182.

Select Bibliography

Al-Adawiyya, Rabi'a. *Doorkeeper of the Heart: Versions of Rabi'a.* Translated by Charles Upton. New York: Pir Press, 2004.

Al-Arabi, Ibn. *Ibn al 'Arabi: The Bezels of Wisdom.* Translated by R. W. J. Austin. Mahwah, NJ: Paulist Press, 1980.

Al-Din Rumi, Jalal. *The Essential Rumi.* Translated by Coleman Barks and John Moyne. New York: HarperOne, 2004.

———. *Mystical Poems of Rumi.* Translated by A. J. Arberry. Chicago: University of Chicago, 1968.

———. *Rumi: The Book of Love. Poems of Ecstasy and Longing.* Translated by Coleman Barks. New York: Harper Collins Publishers, 2003.

Ariel, David S. *Kabbalah: The Mystic Quest in Judaism.* Lanham, MD: Rowman & Littlefield Publishers, 2005).

———. *Mystic Quest: An Introduction to Jewish Mysticism.* New York: Schocken Books, 1992.

Austin, R. W. J. *Sufis of Andalusia.* London: George Allen & Unwin Publishers, 1971.

Bass, Diana Butler. *Christianity after Religion: The End of Church and the Birth of a New Spiritual Awakening.* New York: HarperOne, 2013.

Besserma, Perle. *Teachings of the Jewish Mystics* (Shambhala Teachings). Boston: Shambhala Publications, 1998.

Buber, Martin. *I and Thou.* New York: Scribner, 2000.

Can, Şefik. *Fundamentals of Rumi's Thought* (2nd ed.). Clifton, NJ: Tughra Books, 2006.

Classics of Western Spirituality (a series of more than 90 volumes of the original writings of universally acknowledged teachers within the Catholic, Protestant, Eastern Orthodox, Jewish, Islamic, and Native American traditions). Mahwah, NJ: Paulist Press.

Dickens, Andrea Janelle. *The Female Mystic: Great Women Thinkers of the Middle Ages.* London: B. Tauris, 2009.

Earle, Mary C. *Julian of Norwich: Selections from Revelations of Divine Love—Annotated & Explained.* Woodstock, VT: Skylight Paths Publishing, 2013.

Eckhart, Meister. *Meister Eckhart: The Essential Sermons, Commentaries, Treatises, and Defense.* Translated by Edmund Colledge and Bernard McGinn. Mahwah, NJ: Paulist Press, 1981.

———. *Meister Eckhart: Teacher and Preacher.* Edited by Bernard McGinn. Mahwah, NJ: Paulist Press, 1986.

Eliade, Mircea. *The Sacred and the Profane: The Nature of Religion.* Translated by Willard R. Trask. New York: Harcourt, Brace & World, Inc., 1957.

Eliade, Mircea. *Myths, Dreams, and Mysteries: The Encounter between Contemporary Faiths and Archaic Realities*. Translated by Philip Mairet. New York: Harper & Row, 1975.

Firestone, Tirzah. *The Receiving: Reclaiming Jewish Women's Wisdom*. New York: Harper-One, 2004.

Fox, Matthew. *The Coming of the Cosmic Christ: The Healing of Mother Earth and the Birth of a Global Renaissance*. San Francisco: Harper & Row, 1988.

————. *Breakthrough: Meister Eckhart's Creation Spirituality in New Translation*. Colorado Springs, CO: Image Books, 1980.

Gülen, Fethullah. *Emerald Hills of the Heart: Key Concepts in the Practice of Sufism* (Vol. 2). Clifton, NJ: The Light, Inc., 2004.

Hammarskjold, Dag. *Markings*. Translated by W. H. Auden and L. Fitzgerald Sjoberg. New York: Vintage (Tra edition), 2006.

Happold, F. C. *Mysticism*. New York: Penguin Books, 1970,

Hart, Mother Columba. *Hadewijch: Complete Works*. Mahwah, NJ: Paulist Press 1980.

Harvey, Andrew. *The Way of Passion: A Celebration of Rumi*. New York: Jeremy Tarcher/Putnam, 2001.

Helminski, Camille Adams. *Women of Sufism: A Hidden Treasure*. Boston: Shambhala Publications, 2001.

Hooper, Richard. *The Essential Mystics, Poets, Saints, and Sages: A Wisdom Treasury*. Charlottesville, VA: Hampton Roads Publishing, 2013.

James, William. *The Varieties of Religious Experience: A Study in Human Nature*. New York: New American Library of World Literature, Inc., 1958.

Matt, Daniel C. *The Essential Kabbalah: The Heart of Jewish Mysticism*. New York: Harper-One, 2009.

McGinn, Bernard. *The Flowering of Mysticism: Men and Women in the New Mysticism: 1200-1350 (The Presence of God)* (Vol. 3). New York: Crossroad Publishing Company, 1998.

————. *The Harvest of Mysticism in Medieval Germany* (*The Presence of God*) (Vol. 4). New York: Crossroad Publishing Company, 2005.

————. *The Mystical Thought of Meister Eckhart: The Man from Whom God Hid Nothing*. New York: Crossroad Publishing Company, 2005.

————. *The Varieties of Vernacular Mysticism: 1350–1550 (The Presence of God)*. New York: Crossroad Publishing Company, 2012.

Merton, Thomas. *Merton & Sufism: The Untold Story. A Complete Compendium*. Edited by Rob Baker and Gray Henry. Louisville, KY: Fons Vitae, 2005.

————. *New Seeds of Contemplation*. New York: New Directions Publishing, 2007.

————. *Thomas Merton: Choosing to Love the World: On Contemplation*. Edited by Jonathan Montaldo. Louisville, CO: Sounds True, 2008.

Moore, Thomas. *A Religion of One's Own: A Guide to Creating a Personal Spirituality in a Secular World*. New York: Gotham, 2014.

Myers, Glenn E. *Seeking Spiritual Intimacy: Journeying Deeper with Medieval Women of Faith*. Nottingham, England: Inter-Varsity Press. 2011.

Mystical Union in Judaism, Christianity, and Islam: An Ecumenical Dialogue. Edited by Moshe Idel and Bernard McGinn. London: Continuum International Publishing Group, 1996.

Mystics, Visionaries, and Prophets: A Historical Anthology of Women's Spiritual Writings. Edited by Shawn Madigan. Minneapolis: Fortress Press, 2001.

Nicholas of Cusa. *The Vision of God*. San Diego, CA: The Book Tree, 1999.

Pseudo-Dionysius. *Pseudo-Dionysius: The Complete Works*. Translated by Paul Rorem. Mahwah, NJ: Paulist Press, 1988.

Rakoczy, Susan. *Great Mystics and Social Justice: Walking on the Two Feet of Love*. Mahwah, NJ: Paulist Press, 2006.

Rocca, Gregory *Mystical Languages of Unsaying. Theological Studies* (Vol. 55, n. 4), 760. (Dec. 1, 1994).

Secret Garden: An Anthology in the Kabbalah. Edited by David Meltzer. Barrytown, NY: Barrytown/Station Hill Press, Inc., 2007.

Seesholtz, Anna Groh. *Friends of God: Practical Mystics of the Fourteenth Century.* Whitefish, MT: Kessinger Publishing, LLC, 2006.

Sells, Michael A. *Mystical Languages of Unsaying.* Chicago: University of Chicago, 1994.

Shah, Idries. *The Sufis.* New York: Anchor/Doubleday, 1971.

Shrader, Douglas W. *"Seven Characteristics of Mystical Experiences."* Honolulu, HI: Annual Hawaii International Conference on Arts and Humanities, 2008.

Shimmel, Annemarie. *Mystical Dimensions of Islam.* Chapel Hill: University of North Carolina, 1975.

Simmons, Philip. *Learning to Fall: The Blessings of an Imperfect Life.* New York: Bantam Books, 2002.

Smith, Huston. *The World's Religions: Our Great Wisdom Traditions.* San Francisco: HarperSanFrancisco, 1991.

———. *Why Religions Matter: The Fate of the Human Spirit in an Age of Disbelief.* San Francisco: HarperSanFrancisco, 2001.

Smith, Margaret. *Muslim Women Mystics: The Life and Work of Rabi'a and Other Women Mystics in Islam* (Great Islamic Thinkers). London: Oneworld Publications, 2001.

Soelle, Dorothee. *The Silent Cry: Mysticism and Resistance.* Translated by Barbara Rumscheidt and Martin Rumscheidt. Minneapolis, MN: Fortress Press, 2001.

Soltes, Ori Z. *Mysticism in Judaism, Christianity, and Islam: Searching for Oneness.* Lanham, MD: Rowman & Littlefield, 2009.

Teasdale, Wayne. *The Mystic Heart: Discovering A Universal Spirituality in the World's Religions.* Novato, CA: New World Library, 2001.

Teilhard de Chardin, Pierre. *The Divine Milieu.* New York: Harper Perennial Modern Classics, 2001.

The Cloud of Unknowing. Edited by Hames Walsh. Mahwah, NJ: Paulist Press, 1981.

The Early Kabbalah. Edited by Joseph Dan. Mahwah, NJ: Paulist Press, 1986.

The Essential Mystics: The Soul's Journey into Truth. Edited by Andrew Harvey. San Francisco: HarperSanFrancisco, 1996.

The Wisdom of the Zohar: An Anthology of Texts. Edited by Isaiah Tishby. Oxford, UK: Littman Library of Jewish Civilization, 1989.

Thich Nhat Hanh, *Living Buddha, Living Christ Riverhead Books,* (New York: Penguin Books, 1995).

Thurman, Howard. *Jesus and the Disinherited.* Boston: Beacon Press, 1996.

———. *Meditations of the Heart.* Boston: Beacon Press, 1999.

Tillich, *Paul. The Courage To Be.* Binghamton, NY: Vail-Ballou Press, 1979.

Underhill, Evelyn. *Mysticism: A Study in Nature and Development of Spiritual Consciousness.* Seattle, WA: CreateSpace Independent Publishing Platform. 2011.

Underhill, Eveyln (intro.). *The Cloud of Unknowing.* London: John M. Walkins Press, 1912.

Wolf, Laibl, *Practical Kabbalah: A Guide to Jewish Wisdom for Everyday Life.* New York: Harmony Books, 1999.

Woods, Richard. *Meister Eckhart: Master of Mystics* (vol. 1). New York: Continuum Int'l Publishing Group, 2011.

Zohar: The Book of Enlightenment. Edited and translated by Daniel Chanan Matt. Mahwah, NJ: Paulist Press, 1983.

Index

Made in the USA
Coppell, TX
20 September 2022

83423125R00100